Environmental Protection in India

Socio-economic Aspects

The Book

Present euphoria for rapid economic development has created enormous pressure on India's natural resources. Forests are subjected to rapid degradation due to growing demand for forest-based inputs for industrial use. Rivers are becoming dumping grounds for industrial wastes, often with toxic materials. Construction of large dams is displacing millions of people from their age-old roots. The development projects are carried out for the prosperity of the poor and the marginalised; but the latter never get benefited by this. Their notion of development is different. They share a unique harmonious relationship with nature.

This book deals with the concepts of environment and development and their relationship and the resultant social movements. It investigates as to how the development process affects not only our environment but also the lives of millions of people whose survival is based on environment. In particular, it explores the origin, development, class dimension and other aspects of the Panidari System and its impact on the social situation, and the fight for its eradication. It also traces the origin and issues related to Subern Rekha Andolan. It examines as to how a large dam threatens the lives of poor people and displaces them from their roots. It also explores the alternate theories of development vis-à-vis environmental protection and their relationship with society.

The Author

Abhay Kumar is presently, lecturer in the Department of Political Science in Shri Ram College of Commerce (SRCC), University of Delhi. The author has contributed numerous articles on environmental and social issues in journals at national level and has closely interacted with social activists on the above issues.

Environmental Protection in India

Socio-economic Aspects

By

Abhay Kumar

New Century Publications
New Delhi, India

NEW CENTURY PUBLICATIONS
4852 / 24, 1st Floor,
Ansari Road, Daryaganj,
New Delhi – 110 002 (India)

Tel.: 98112 66355; 011-4101 7798; 4358 7398
E-mail: info@newcenturypublications.com

www.newcenturypublications.com

Editorial office:
4800 / 24, Bharat Ram Road,
Ansari Road, Daryaganj,
New Delhi – 110 002

Edition: 2026

ISBN: **978-81-7708-093-3**

Published by New Century Publications and printed at Milan Enterprises, New Delhi.

Designs: Patch Creative Unit, New Delhi.

PRINTED IN INDIA

Preface

This work is a result of my long association with many individuals and institutions. I met late Anil Agarwal, noted Indian environmentalist, and had the opportunity to work with him. My association with him and his organisation Centre for Science and Environment (CSE) exposed me to issues like development, environment, large dams and other developmental projects which cause harm to the environment and pose a survival threat for the poor, women and tribals. The CSE in its annual report "The State of India's Environment: The First Citizen's Report" (1982) covered almost all environmental movements which took place at that time. What do our policy makers think about the development is different and how the concerned people for whom the development is imposed, view it. The development projects are always carried out for the prosperity of the poor and the marginalised; but the latter never get benefited by this. Their notion of development is different. They share a unique harmonious relationship with nature. In the subsequent pages, it has been tried to explore this peculiar dichotomy and how to resolve it.

This work is organised into 5 chapters, Besides, there are 2 appendices which provide supplementary information on the subject. Chapter 1 is introductory in nature, explaining the legal and institutional framework for environmental protection in India. It also traces the evolution of social movements against environmental degradation in India. Chapter 2 deals with the concepts of environment, development and their relationship and the resultant social movements. It investigates as to how the development process affects not only our environment but also the lives of millions of people whose survival is based on environment. Chapter 3 explores the origin, development, class dimension and other aspects of the Panidari System and its impact on the social situation, and the fight for its eradication. Chapter 4 is devoted to the origin and issues related to Subern Rekha Andolan. It examines as to how a large dam threatens the lives of poor people and displaces them from their roots. Chapter 5 explores the alternative theories of development vis-à-vis environmental protection and their relationship with society.

I take this opportunity to thank individuals who have over the years shaped my intellectual interests and ideas. I am greatly indebted to Professor Susheela Kaushik, Professor S.K. Chaube, Professor Neera Chandhok, Professor Manoranjan Mohanty and Dr. Shanta N. Varma for their help and encouragement.

I am grateful to Shri Smitu Kothari, Shri Rajendra Ravi, Shri Ghanshyam, Shri Anil Prakash, Shri Kumar Chandra Mardi and many more activists of the Swarn Rekha Andolan. A special mention of Shri Surendra Biruli is highly needed. He provided me some rare documents and papers from his personal files, made many activists available for discussions and spared lot of time for me.

I am also thankful to Mr. Sandeep Sury, Chief Executive of M/S New Century Publications, New Delhi for his immense help and favour to publish this book.

Delhi **Abhay Kumar**

Contents

1

Government Policies and Social Awareness for the Protection of Environment

1.1 Introduction

Human intervention in the process of social change has taken many forms of politics. In India the spectrum of politics continues to widen. In addition to the traditional patterns of organised politics, there has been a surge of popular democratic movements. Appropriately there has been a growing intellectual interest in this phenomenon.

After independence in 1947 people had great expectations from the indigenous government. It was assumed that the new government which was more aware of the Indian problems and was equally concerned for the people would definitely seek to eradicate all the problems. With the installation of the new government under the leadership of Nehru with the objectives of modernisation and industrialisation, raised hopes. Even though the new experiment started very enthusiastically, gradually people started feeling disappointed and frustrated.

Modernisation and industrialisation affect nature in two ways. Firstly, it is extremely destructive of the environment in its search for inexpensive biomass-based raw materials, and for the opportunities for waste disposal. In the absence of strong laws which are equally strongly implemented, there is no internalisation of environmental costs and both public sector units and private industrialists prefer to pass them on to society.

Secondly, modernisation is steadily transforming the very character of nature. In physical terms, the tendency is to reduce the diversity in nature and transform it into high-yielding monocultures. The driving force for this transformation arises out of the commodification of nature. Maximum production and maximum profit is the aim.

The effect of the massive environmental change taking place in India has been disastrous for the people. India is an extremely poor country with a high level of population density. There is no ecological space left in the physical environment today which is not occupied by one human group or another for its sustenance. In the name of economic development, often, any human activity which results in the destruction of an ecological space or in its transformation, is justified.

The post-independence political debate in India has centred on two major issues: equity and growth. The environmental concern has added a third dimension: sustainability. India's biggest challenge today is to identify and implement a development process that will lead to greater equity, growth and sustainability.

The environment is not just pretty trees and tigers, threatened plants and ecosystems. It is literally the entity on which we all subsist, and on which entire agricultural and industrial development depends. Development can take place at the cost of the environment only up to a point. Development without concern for the environment can only be short-term development. In the long term, it can be anti-development and can go on at the cost of enormous human suffering, increased poverty, oppression and marginalisation.

1.2 Current State of Environment in India

India is the second most populous and seventh largest country in the world. It has a land frontier of 15,200 kilometres and its sea coast runs to the length of 6,100 kilometres. As regards its biological diversity, over 45,000 plant species are found in the country. The vascular flora which form the conspicuous vegetation cover itself comprises about 15,000 species. Several thousands of them are endemic to this country and they have so far not been reported from anywhere in the world. The biological diversity of the country is so rich that it may play a very important and crucial role in future for the survival of entire mankind, if it is conserved with utmost care.

After achieving Independence from Britain in 1947, India launched an ambitious programme of economic development focused on the provision of basic human needs of food, shelter, health, education and employment. The colonial exploitation had left the country much backward in all spheres of life. Agriculture was stagnant, industrialisation poor and lop-sided, means of transport and communications underdeveloped, and social security schemes non-existent. Consequently, death-rate was high, poverty rampant and unemployment widespread.

The country embarked on a programme of planned economic development with the launching of First Five Year Plan in 1951. Ever since, the emphasis has been on removal of poverty and unemployment and all possible instruments of economic policy have been used to achieve the twin-objectives.

However, the euphoria for rapid economic development created enormous pressure on country's natural resources. Forests were subjected to rapid degradation due to growing demand for forest-based inputs for industrial use. Other natural resources, namely water, land, and air became dumping grounds for industrial wastes, often with toxic materials. In short, environmental issues were completely overlooked during the first two decades (1950-70) of economic development.

It was in the early 1970s that Government realised the need for environmental protection as an integral part of industrial policy. Unfortunately, considerable damage had already been done to India's natural resources by the time preventive measures were taken. Thus, land/soil degradation has taken place due to floods, waterlogging, salination, indiscriminate mining and faulty agricultural practices. Similarly, forest wealth is dwindling due to withdrawal of forest products (timber, fuel wood), overgrazing, forest fires and location of development projects in forest areas.

Furthermore, noise levels in urban areas of India are excessively high due to rise in population, automobiles and industrial activities. The ambient air quality of major cities and towns in the country is being monitored under the National Ambient Air Quality Monitoring (NAAQM) programme. The monitoring results indicate that sulphur dioxide and nitrogen dioxide levels are mostly within the permissible limits whereas Suspended Particulate Matter (SPM) values are higher than the prescribed limits at some places due to vehicular and air pollution, burning of fossil fuel and natural dusty conditions. The pollution caused by vehicles contributes significantly towards air pollution. Similarly, the data on ambient water quality of rivers indicates that levels of coliform count and Biological Oxygen Demand (BOD) are generally high resulting in deterioration of water quality. This is primarily due to inadequate sanitation facilities and discharge of waste water into the surface water bodies without proper treatment. The dangers of environmental pollution are well-known. Thus, mercury poisoning results in neurological afflictions and exposure to toxic materials causes acute illness or even death.

The damage done to India's environment over the last five decades or so has been enormous. Ecological damage is often irreversible. Cleaning up later is not an option when terrestrial and aquatic biodiversity has been lost because of habitat destruction. For example, pollution and destructive fishing techniques have damaged a large proportion of coral reefs in some areas. As up to one-fourth of all marine species and one-fifth of known marine fish species live in coral reef ecosystems, the loss of reef habitats disproportionately threatens a high percentage of the ocean's plant and animal life. Complete reversal of this damage is unlikely; therefore, efforts need to focus on preserving global biological resources before they are damaged.

1.3 Causes of Environmental Degradation

Environmental degradation in India has been caused by a variety of social, economic, institutional and technological factors. Rapidly growing population, urbanisation, industrial activities and increasing use of pesticides and fossil fuels have all resulted in considerable deterioration in the quality and sustainability of the environment.

After China, India is the most populous country in the world accounting for 16.0 per cent of world population and having only 2.4 per cent of total world area. India's population has increased rapidly since Independence. It increased from 36.1 crore in 1951 to 43.9 crore in 1961, to 54.8 crore in 1971 and to 68.5 crore in 1981. The census of 1991 enumerated the population at 84.4 crore which increased to 102.7 crore in 2001 It is expected to be 116.4 crore in the year 2011. The rapidly growing population has adversely affected environment through the excessive use of arable land, forests and water resources besides the production of wastes.

India's growing population has aggravated the problems of poverty and unemployment. Poverty is said to be both cause and effect of environmental degradation. The circular link between poverty and environment is an extremely complex phenomenon. Inequality may foster unsustainability because the poor, who rely on natural resources more than the rich, deplete natural resources faster as they have no real prospects of gaining access to other types of resources. Moreover, degraded environment can accelerate the process of impoverishment, again because the poor depend directly on natural assets. Similarly, lack of employment opportunities in rural areas are driving the rural poor to metropolitan cities, creating urban slums and the problems associated with them.

1.4 Government Policies and Initiatives

Natural and environmental resources are the basis of all economic activities. Soil, forests, mines, water, air and other natural resources are productive assets of an economy. In fact, productivity of an economic system depends to a large extent on the supply and quality of its natural resources. Poor quality of water and air adversely affect the health of population, causing reduced labour productivity and premature mortality. Similarly, soil degradation and erosion leads to reduced and inferior quality agricultural output.

Economic activities in turn affect the quantity and quality of natural and environmental resources. Mining, lumbering, manufacturing, fishing and a host of other economic activities change the stock of natural resources. The change of stock calls for appropriate trade-off between the needs of present and future generations. Economic growth without environmental considerations can cause serious damage to the quality of life of the present and future generations.

Economists distinguish between economic growth and economic development. Economic growth means sustained increase in per capita real income. Economic development is a much wider term. It includes economic growth and at the same time encompasses questions regarding patterns of production, distribution of national income, consumption behaviour of the people and concern for environment.

The concept of sustainable development advocates economic progress in an environmentally responsible manner. Sustainable development attempts to strike a balance between the demands of the economic development and the need for protection of the environment. It seeks to combine the elements of economic efficiency, intergenerational equity, social concerns and environmental protection. Although, the term sustainable development has many interpretations, it generally refers to non-declining human well-being over time.

1.4.1 Protection of Environment as a Fundamental Duty: Part IV of the Constitution of India contains Directive Principles of State Policy. Article 48A of the Constitution falling under Part IV states

"The State shall endeavour to protect and improve the environment and to safeguard the forests and wildlife of the country".

Similarly, Part IVA of the Constitution, inserted by the Constitution (Forty-second Amendment) Act, 1976, contains Fundamental Duties of every citizen of India. Article 51A (g) of the Constitution falling under Part IVA states

"It shall be the duty of every citizen of India to protect and improve the natural environment including forests, lakes, rivers and wildlife, and to have compassion for living creatures".

1.4.2 Legislative Measures: Problems related to environment received direct attention of the Government in the Fourth Five Year Plan (1969-74) and a Committee was set up in 1972 to look into these problems and suggest solutions. Another Committee was set up in January 1980 for reviewing the existing legislative measures and administrative machinery for ensuring environmental protection. Following the recommendations of this Committee, the Department of Environment was set up in 1980 which was upgraded to a full-fledged Ministry of Environment and Forests in 1985.

Presently, there are about 30 major enactments related to protection of environment being administered by the Central and State Governments. The prominent among these are the following:

1. The Wildlife (Protection) Act, 1972
2. The Water (Prevention and Control of Pollution) Act, 1974.
3. The Water (Prevention and Control of Pollution) Cess Act, 1977.
4. The Forest Conservation Act, 1980.
5. The Air (Prevention and Control of Pollution) Act, 1981.
6. The Environment Protection Act, 1986.
7. The Motor Vehicle Act, 1938 (as amended in 1988).
8. The Public Liability Insurance Act, 1991.

1.4.3 Institutional Framework: The foregoing legislations have empowered the Central and State Governments to create necessary institutions and instruments to prevent environmental degradation. These legislations are implemented through several organisations, mainly through Pollution Control Boards at the Central and State levels. Thus, stringent norms for vehicular emissions were notified under the Central Motor Vehicles Rules which came into force in April 1996. Supply of unleaded petrol in four metropolitan cities of Mumbai, Calcutta, Delhi and Chennai was introduced from April 1, 1995 for use in four wheel vehicles fitted with catalytic converters. Government has plans to gradually expand the use of unleaded petrol to other cities in the country.

The Ministry of Environment and Forests is the nodal agency at the Central level for planning, promoting, and co-ordinating the environmental schemes and programmes. The executive responsibility for prevention and control of industrial pollution lies primarily with the Central Pollution Control Board. At the State level, the designated agencies for this purpose are the State Pollution Control Boards.

If a proposed industrial unit is likely to discharge effluents into a stream, sewer, or on land, it is required to obtain a 'Consent to Establish' for discharge of effluents under the Water (Prevention and Control of Pollution) Act, 1974. Similarly, if the proposed unit is to be located in an air pollution control area as declared by the concerned State Government, and is likely to emit any air pollutants in the atmosphere, it is required to obtain a "Consent to Establish" for emission under the Air (Prevention and Control of Pollution) Act, 1981.

Prior environment clearance has been made mandatory for 29 specified categories of development projects through a statutory notification issued in January 1994. The underlying purpose is to mitigate the adverse environmental effects of these projects and in integrating the environmental concerns into development.

The Central Pollution Control Board is the national apex body for assessment, monitoring, and control of water and air pollution. The Board has identified 17 categories of heavily polluting industries, namely cement, thermal power plants, distilleries, sugar, fertiliser, integrated iron and steel, oil refineries, pulp and paper, petrochemicals, pesticides, tanneries, basic drugs and pharmaceuticals, dye and dye intermediates, caustic soda, zinc smelter, copper smelter, and aluminium smelter. According to the data collected by the Central Pollution Control Board (CPCB) on September 30, 1996, out of 1,551 units belonging to 17 categories of highly polluting industries, 1,259 units had facilities to comply with the environmental standards, 112 were closed and 180 were not having adequate facilities. Show cause notices under Section 5 of the Environment (Protection) Act, 1986 have been issued to all the defaulting units.

In February 1992, the Ministry of Environment and Forests announced a policy statement for abatement of pollution. It emphasised pollution prevention through adoption of best available clean and practicable technologies rather than end of the pipe treatment. In other words, the focus is on source reduction, and substitution of chemicals with safe alternatives.

National Environmental Tribunal Act, which came into force from June 17, 1995, provides relief, compensation, and restitution to victims of accidents while handling hazardous substances, and for environmental damages. Similarly, National Environment Appellate Authority (NEAA), set up by the Government in January 1997 facilitates public hearing into the environment impact assessment. NEAA is expected to ensure greater transparency and faster decision-making in matters concerning the environmental impact of industrial projects. Furthermore, Government has launched an Eco-Mark scheme to certify various products of the industries which fulfil the prescribed pollution control standards to achieve the objective of environment-friendly production, packaging and waste disposal.

1.4.4 Financial Assistance:

1. Under the Scheme for Promotion of Common Effluent Treatment Plants in clusters of small industries (aided by World Bank), financial assistance towards capital investment up to 50 per cent or Rs. 1 crore, whichever is less, is given as a subsidy.

2. Central Government assistance up to 40 per cent or a maximum of Rs. 1.5 crore is provided for setting up demonstration projects in the areas of waste minimisation, clean technologies, and waste recycling.

3. Assistance is provided to large and medium scale units to install effluent treatment plants aimed at waste minimisation, resource recovery, and pollution abatement.

1.4.5 Fiscal Incentives

A. Income Tax: Income tax concessions for environmental purposes are provided under Section 35 CCB of the Indian Income Tax Act, 1961. These concessions are available to taxpayers carrying on business or profession. They are of the following types.

1. Sums paid by a taxpayer to any association or institution, which has as its object the undertaking of programmes of conservation of natural resources, to be used for such programmes, are allowed as deductions in the computation of taxable profits. The deduction under this provision is not allowed unless the association or institution, as also the programme of conservation of natural resources for which such sums are paid have been approved by the prescribed authority (i.e. Secretary, Department of Environment, Government of India). The prescribed authority will not approve an association or institution for this purpose for more than three years at a time.

2. Sums paid to an association or institution which has as its object the undertaking of any programme of afforestation are allowed as deduction in the computation of taxable profits. For this purpose, both the association/institution and the programme of afforestation will have to be approved by the prescribed authority.

3. Any payment made to a notified Fund for Afforestation will also qualify for deduction under section 35 CCB. A National Fund for Afforestation and Wasteland Development has been set up. Donations from individuals as well as corporate/non-corporate bodies are eligible for 100 per cent deduction.

Long-term Capital Gains: Under Section 54G of the Indian Income Tax Act, 1961, long-term capital gains made from the transfer of machinery, plant, land, and building etc., forming part of an industrial undertaking are exempt from taxation where transfer is effected for the shifting of the industrial undertaking from an urban area to any other area, provided these are reinvested in approved relocation schemes within one year before or three years after the date of transfer. The amount of exemption is equal to the amount so utilised or the amount of capital gains, whichever is less. Apparently, the purpose of this exemption is to encourage industries to shift out of congested urban areas to reduce pollution and other hazards.

Depreciation Allowance: Depreciation allowance at the rate of 100 per cent is granted for installing pollution control equipment. Pollution control equipment has been given the benefit of accelerated depreciation for corporate tax computation. In the 1993-94 budget, 100 per cent of written down capital cost of such equipment is exempted from the corporate tax.

In his 1998-99 budget, the Finance Minister allowed 100 per cent deduction, subject to a ceiling of Rs. 5 lakh, to undertakings engaged in the collection or processing of biodegradable waste. Similarly, activities which encourage the production of bacteria induced fertilisers were made eligible for 100 per cent deduction under Section 35AC of the Income Tax Act.

B. Excise Duty Concessions:

1. Production of building material using fly ash and phosphogypsum in 25 per cent or more quantities as raw material is exempt from excise duty.

2. Bricks and tiles manufactured using red mud in 25 per cent or more quantities as raw material are exempt from excise duty.

3. Excise duty at the low rate of 5 per cent is levied on manufactured goods that are used for pollution control.

C. Customs Duty Concessions: Customs waive off is provided by the Government to encourage the installation of appropriate pollution abatement equipment.

1. Exemption from customs duty is allowed on the import of equipment, machinery, and capital goods required for the production of building materials, using fly ash/phosphogypsum, such as bricks, light weight aggregates and light weight concrete elements.

2. Customs duty is levied at the reduced rate of 35 per cent on equipment and spares for pollution control.

3. Customs duty is levied at the reduced rate of 25 per cent on kits required for conversion of petrol driven vehicles to compressed natural gas driven vehicles.

As a measure of environmental protection, the Finance Minister in his 1998-99 budget reduced the import duty on sawn wood and certain other varieties of wood from 30 per cent to 25 per cent, on biopesticides (which are eco-friendly) from 30 per cent to 5 per cent and on membrane electrolysers and parts from 25 per cent to 10 per cent.

1.5 Ninth Five Year Plan (1997-2002) and Environment

India's Ninth Five Year Plan (1997-2002) gave considerable importance to the protection of the environment in its development strategy. The policy on environment was guided by the principles of Agenda 21 which was adopted at the Earth Summit in Rio de Janeiro in June 1992 and which aims at integrating environmental imperatives with developmental aspirations. The principles of Agenda 21 find reflection in the policy statements of the Government of India on forestry, abatement of pollution, national conservation strategy and environment and development. India is a signatory to the Montreal Protocol for phasing out ozone depleting substances, the Convention on biological diversity and other international treaties.

1.5.1 Approach Paper to the Ninth Plan: In the Approach Paper to the Ninth Five Year Plan, environmental conservation and protection was an important component of development programmes in all the sectors of the economy. It provided for as follows.

- To carry out studies on carrying capacity in environmentally fragile areas of the country. A proper legislative and institutional framework to be evolved for the protection of such areas which are endangered.
- To formulate a time bound inventorisation programme of the flora and fauna of all the regions of the country.
- Establishment of Natural Resource Management Groups by the States at the district level to closely monitor the state of the environment.
- Reorganisation of various environmental regulatory agencies to become self-supportive.
- Motivating industry through incentives to be responsive to environmental protection measures.
- Involvement of local *Panchayati Raj* institutions and the

community at large in implementing environmental protection programmes and bringing about environmental awareness.
- Net-working of existing institutions for identification of pollution sources and prevention of pollution.

According to the Approach Paper, "The total geographical area of the country is 3.28 million sq. kms. The total forest area in the country is 0.76 million sq. kms. which constitutes 23.2 per cent of the total geographical area (The percentage of actual forest to geographical area is 19.5). According to the National Forest Policy (1988), 33 per cent of the total geographical area of the country should be under forest cover. However, the present level of forest cover is much lower than desired." [1] Hence, "Regeneration of the forest cover is an important component of environmental sustainability. This not only requires attention to the preservation of existing forests, particularly in the fragile eco-regions of the Himalayas and the *Ghats* among others, but also a greater effort to create forest cover in a widespread manner. It is proposed that every district in the country should reserve at least 2 per cent of its available area as forest." [2]

1.5.2 Ninth Plan Final Document: In order to ensure environmental sustainability of the development process, the final document of the Ninth Plan envisaged a multi-pronged strategy the important elements of which were as under.

- Empowering the people through information generation, dissemination and access.
- Involving the industry in both the private and the public sector.
- Integrating environment with decision making through valuation of environmental impacts; evolving market based economic instruments as an alternative to the command and control form of environmental regulation; appropriate pricing of natural resources based on their long-term marginal cost of supply; appropriate fiscal reforms and natural resource accounting.
- Evolving the rights for common property resources.
- Inter-sectoral co-ordination and co-operation.

- Ensuring scientific and technological inputs.
- Participation of people (particularly women) in the management and sharing of usufruct through Joint Forest Management.
- Involvement of NGOs for awareness building and as an interface between forest department and the people would be encouraged during the Ninth Plan.
- Integrated development of villages in and around forests.

1.6 Tenth Five Year Plan (2002-07) on Environment

Expressing dissatisfaction with the implementation of environmental schemes and laws, the Tenth Plan observed, "The major instrument with the States to check environmental degradation is undoubtedly regulation. The country has adopted almost all environmental protection Acts and Rules enforced in developed countries. But environmental degradation continues despite the existence of a long-standing policy, and legal-cum-institutional framework for environmental protection. The need for reducing the gap between principle and practice cannot be over-emphasised. [3] The Plan Document suggested, *inter alia,* the following two measures to check environmental degradation.

- Environmental clearance of projects by State Pollution Control Boards takes a long time. There is a need for standardisation of procedures and setting of time frames.
- For control of industrial pollution, limits on effluent discharge have been laid down. An economic instrument can also be introduced to force the industry to move towards zero discharge. Industry should be made to pay higher penalty if its effluent discharge contains a higher level of pollutants

In India, Government has taken various measures, preventive as well as promotive, to improve environment. However, it has not used pollution taxes for environmental protection. The currently levied cess on the consumption of water for industrial activities is not a pollution tax. Its objective is to raise revenue for the pollution control boards but not to control pollution. Pollution taxes are levied in many countries with public support. Thus,

Brazil, Colombia, and Venezuela charge a forestry tax when tree harvesting is not compensated by equivalent reforestation. Similarly, landfill tax is imposed in many Western countries including Britain.

The policy in India has focused on providing pollution subsidies (i.e. tax concessions) to industries in various forms. These subsidies have not proved effective in controlling pollution. They do not force the polluters, as do pollution taxes, to adopt pollution abatement technologies. Similarly, there has been a lack of an appropriate price policy for the use of natural resources. The Approach Paper to the Ninth Five Year Plan has lamented this fact as follows, "The most important methodology for preventing undue depletion of natural resources is by ensuring their efficient use at all levels. This has two important dimensions: First, exhaustible or vulnerable natural resources should be priced appropriately in order to prevent over-exploitation. In India, since a large proportion of natural resources are subjected to administered prices, there has been a tendency to under-price resources quite significantly. This approach needs to be changed urgently. Second, technologies which conserve the use of natural resources need to be developed and promoted vigorously." [4]

To clean up the polluted rivers in the country, River Action Plans were started in phases. Many of these remain incomplete even after ten years of their inception. Out of the total sanctioned 261 schemes, some are incomplete due to serious problems relating to contractual matters, technology selection, cost overruns etc. Even in case of the completed schemes, the created assets are in a dilapidated state, needing repair work. The question of operation and maintenance of these assets after the completion of the schemes still remains unsettled.

1.7 Social Awareness and Movements

Today in India the main concern of the environment movement is about the use of the environment – how should the environment be used and who should use it and benefit from it. Such a concern is the result of a growing understanding of the relationship between the people and their environment, born out of a concern for a more equitable and sustainable use of the environment.

The nature of environment movement in India is based on access to economic resources. In India the entire environment movement is linked to the question of survival. The Chipko movement, Tehri dam movement, Koel-Karo in the east, Sirsi in the South, Subern Rekha Andolan and Ganga Mukti Andolan of Bihar and the likes are based on the issue of survival of the people.

These were some of the grass root environment movements which emerged in the 1970's. These were searching for a new kind of peace – peace with nature. In spite of differences in the stage and in the actors, these movements shared the common objective of a search for an alternative development. Alternative, here implies a radical-democratic and humanistic critique of modern industrial society, of contemporary modernisation/ industrialisation strategies, and of the dominant oppositional ideologies and institutions.

In 1970s and 1980s many social movements started in different parts of the country. Some of them were based on social-political issues and others on the question of people's livelihood and related with issue of environment. This study aims to analyse the very concepts of development and environment and their relationship. At times such a relationship is in the nature of an antagonistic one, it is then that social movements take place. For the purpose of analysing these issues, two environmental movements have been taken as case studies.

Environment movements are mainly linked to the question of human survival and livelihood, in addition to raising issues of pollution and environmental degradation. If we do not care for environment and blindly follow a kind of development which is not indigenous and suitable for local situations, it will create problems in civil society.

The concern with environment and development is significant in the intellectual necessity of redefining the whole purpose of development. It will entail the search for an alternative model of development based on something that is at once more comprehensive and more accessible to all human beings. He suggests that each and every society must evolve its own alternative and that the alternatives before man in society are infinite. The concept of alternatives, then, is not to be limited just to development policies, it should entail visions about society and polity, and it should do this in the context of the evolution of the human community as a whole. The movement towards an alternative model of development should apply to all regions of the world, whether developing or developed, and that it should combine in its framework both a sustainable process of development, through a continuous regeneration of renewable resources, and a reduction in resource and income disparities between and within regions.

Rajni Kothari suggests some basic postulates in the conception of an alternative pattern of development like removal of poverty, equity through local self- reliance, self-reliance and decentralization, endogenous science.

Anil Agarwal in his edited book *The Fight For Survival* says that environmental destruction in India threatens the very survival of millions of poor people. He further says that India is too poor a country to neglect its environment- the survival base of its poor citizens, indeed their fundamental right. The worst sufferers of the environmental degradation are the country's poor because they do not benefit much from the Gross National Product. They survive because of the Gross Nature Product. According to him waste and want are the two greatest problems of our time. It is the affluent who are the biggest polluters and destroyers of the environment. He suggests three objectives before the country's development process: Growth, Equity, and sustainability. He further suggests some action plan for environmental protection like protection of natural resources from irrational pressure of development, environmentally–sound planning built around concepts of equity and sustainability, employment guarantee built around programmes for ecological regeneration, rural development must become equitous and holistic enrichment of village ecosystems, resource-rational urbanization, conservation- oriented education and a national rehabilitation policy. He concludes that the state of the environment and the human condition are closely related to each other. Environmental degradation and social injustice are two sides of the same coin.

According to Vandana Shiva development have been a post-colonial project, a choice for accepting a model of progress in which the entire world remade itself on the model of the colonizing modern west .Development, as the improved well-being of all, was thus equated with the westernization of economic categories – of needs, of productivity, of growth. In her book *Staying Alive* she argues that development was reduced to a continuation of the process of colonization, it became an extension of the project of wealth creation in modern western patriarchy's economic vision, which was based on the exploitation or exclusion of women on the exploitation and degradation of nature, and on the exploitation and erosion of other cultures. Economic growth was a new colonialism, draining resources away from those who needed them most.

The displacement of women from productive activity by the expansion of development was rooted largely in the manner in which development projects appropriated or destroyed the natural resource base for the production of sustenance and survival. She further argues that in the market economy, the organizing principle for natural resource use is the maximization of profits and capital accumulation. Nature and human needs are managed through market mechanism. She says that the old assumption that with the development process the availability of goods and services will automatically be increased and poverty will be removed, is now under serious challenge from women's ecology movements in the third world. Gail Omvedt in her writings opines that Indian environmental movements are most strongly based among peasants and adivasis, and that their fight for livelihood on the issues of forests, famine and fishing not only confronts the state but also raises new issues about the nature of economic development itself and the very meaning of socialism. Ramchandra Guha has written enough on environment but most of his writings are related with history of different environment movements. He has written a book *Unquiet Woods* on Chipko movement. His other writing *This Fissured Land* traces the origin and history of environment movements in India. His other writings discusses different ideologies and other aspects of the environment and reasons for the environment movements in the country.

According to Shekhar Singh it is unfortunate that even today issues relating to the natural environment are not usually considered important enough to form a central part of the debates on political economy. Whenever the debate has started, it has usually been seen as a debate of development versus environment, as if economic and development issues are so to speak on one side and environmental issues in opposition to it. He says that the legitimate environmental debate does not lie in contradiction with issues of economic development, but rather ought to be seen as an integral part of the questions of development. Darryl D'Monte opposes the western model of development which causes harm to the environment. He also favours the idea that there should be a synthesis between development and environment. Smitu Kothari also talks about a sustainable development which should take care of environment. In this way different social scientists, environmentalists and social activists have expressed their view points about development and environment.

1.8 Origin of Environment Movements in India

There is a dominant understanding that the Indian environmental movements started in early 1970s. However, there is another school of thought which locate the movement's origin in Indira Gandhi's famous speech on 'poverty and pollution' at the 1972 Stockholm Conference. There are still others, mainly activists who point out that Chipko Andolan is the beginning of environmental movement in India. But Ramchandra Guha, a noted environmentalist says that Indian environmentalism did not begin either with Indira Gandhi or Chipko.

If we analyse the Indian environmental movements, three different ideological perspectives are visible among them. It is quite possible that none of these ideologies is present in a particular movement or of all the three may be present in some.

The first strand, which is inspired from Gandhian philosophy, relies heavily on a religious idiom in its rejection of the modern way of life. The followers of this approach have literally taken Gandhi's invocation of Ram Rajya. The methods of protest practised by this group have roots in Gandhism–*fasts, padayatras, satyagrahas* and *poojas*.

The second strand can be termed Appropriate Technology. It works for a working synthesis of agriculture and industry, big and small units and western and eastern technological traditions. It is influenced by western liberalism. Their emphasis is not so much on challenging the system, as in demonstrating in practice a set of technological and social alternatives to the present model of urban-industrial development.

The third strand has its roots in Marxism. They have been termed as Ecological Marxism. They are perhaps most closely identified with the Peoples Science Movements whose basic concern with 'taking science to the people' has widened to include environmental protection.

1.9 Chipko: Pioneer in Indian Environment Movement

Without mentioning of the Chipko movement, the description of India's environmental movement is not complete. Chipko movement started in early 1973 when forest department tried its best to cut down the trees in hilly districts of Uttrakhand. Under the leadership of Chandi Prasad Bhatt, villagers suddenly thought of embracing the trees. Thus 'Chipko' (to hug) was born. The villagers of Mandal village resolved to hug the trees even if axes split open their stomachs. Chipko movement provided fuel to most of the social movements in India. There were several reasons for this. Chipko was indigenous and not inspired by any international experiment. It was a by-product of self-motivated peasants out of their survivalhood. Secondly, its historic and cultural associations were easily identifiable; its methods and techniques were completely non-violent and inspired by Gandhian methodology. Third, Chipko articulated a truly social ecology; it raised questions of equity and justice. And finally, and most importantly, Chipko was representative of a spectrum of natural resource conflicts that erupted in many parts of India in the 1970s and 1980s. These conflicts were of different nature : for access to forests, fish and grazing resources, conflicts for access to land, food and water over the construction of large dams and the effects of industrial pollution.

India's environment movements are searching for justice and peace through a restructuring of man's relationship with nature. In India, the balance between nature's productivity and people's needs is a delicate one. Environment movements in India are, by and large, struggles by or on behalf of the dispossessed, the marginalised and the non-commercial farmers. These movements are aimed at conserving nature's balance in order to conserve the means of survival of the poor.

1.10 Two Case Studies: Ganga Mukti Andolan and Subern Rekha Andolan

The two social movements called Ganga Mukti Andolan and Subern Rekha Andolan were organised for the fisherfolk and tribals respectively. Ganga Mukti Andolan fought against the panidari (water lordism). It was like zamindari system which was imposed on the use of water. This system was prevalent in the Bhagalpur district of Bihar. Due to its exploitative nature, thousands of fisherfolk migrated to other places. Most of those who stayed back were in precarious social conditions. This movement fought for their cause and was able to a great extent to provide freedom to fisherfolk for free fishing rights.

Subern Rekha Andolan came into existence as a protest movement against the construction of a large dam on the river Subern Rekha near Ranchi in Jharkhand. Its objectives were: to provide water supply for irrigation to Jharkhand, Orissa and West Bengal; to provide water for municipal and industrial use to Jamshedpur steel city, to reduce flood damages in Orissa and West Bengal and to produce electricity for public consumption. After completion of the dam about 37,600 people would have been displaced from Chandil reservoir territory alone. This is besides other reservoirs, the number of people to be displaced was much larger. So the local people, mainly tribals, protested against this.

Notes

1. Government of India, Planning Commission, *Approach Paper to the Ninth Five Year Plan*, p. 63.
2. *Ibid.*, p. 35.
3. Government of India, Planning Commission, *Tenth Five Year Plan (2002-07)*, Volume II, p. 1075.
4. *Approach paper to the Ninth Five Year Plan, op. cit.,* 36.

2

Development, Environment and Social Movements

Economic development and sound environmental management are complementary aspects of the same agenda. Without adequate environmental protection, development will be undermined; without development, environmental protection will fail, as economic growth is essential for sustained poverty reduction. But growth has often caused serious environmental damage.

2.1 Sustainable Economic Development

The French sociologist Raymond Aron has cited three interpretations of what development may constitute. In the first place, it is the long term statistical trend of economic growth. Alternately, it is the contrast between rich and the poor countries. Both these views are incorporated in the "stages of growth" theory propagated by W.W. Rostow. In his theory, development is a linear path along which all the countries travel. At various stages in history, if the advanced countries reached the stage of "take-off" earlier; the poor countries or at least the more fortunate among them will approach it in due course. If they do not, it is because, in Rostow's view they lack capital, technology, expertise and motivation. A third interpretation of the process and one which applies only to the west and that too only during the cold war period, is the gap between affluent capitalist countries and the Soviet bloc. The actual technologies which make societies develop are socially and culturally determined; in turn, these technologies transform the societies.

Most planners in third world countries have their schooling in welfare economics which, as the economist Sanjay Lall points out, "furnished the paradigm within which conventional development economists operate. This also provides for social cost benefit analysis which, together with development economics, provides welfare theory, in Lall's view, "the meaning of the language used, the value judgements adhered to, the questions asked, and the methods used for interpreting the answers found." [1] A high rate of gross national product is associated with rapid consumption and hence high social welfare.

The well-known Pakistani economist, Mahabubul Haq articulated it well at an international development conference in 1972. "Developing countries have no choice but to turn inwards and adopt a different style more consistent with their own poverty". Development goals should be elimination of malnutrition, disease, illiteracy, squalor, unemployment and inequality". They should not be merely concerned with how much is produced, but what is produced and how it is distributed ---- this requires a redefinition of economic and social objectives --- of truly staggering proportions."

Professor Amulya Kumar Reddy, head of the cell for the Application of Science and Technology to Rural Areas (ASTRA) at the Indian Institute of Science at Bangalore has been arguing with passion for precisely such an approach and has been drawing attention to the potential of alternative technology. Central to what would comprise genuine development, in his scheme of things, is the index how much energy a person consumes, rather than his per capita income, this comprises both calories in the shape of food and other external forms like fuel for cooking and lighting.

Reddy has been doing seminal work at ASTRA, identifying alternative sources of energy. His scenario is to see energy as a component of a development strategy which does three things – it satisfies human needs starting with the needs of the neediest; it is directed towards indigenous self reliance and it is in harmony with the environment. In other words, it views development from the base upwards, instead of expecting the benefits to trickle downwards.

Economists like Dandekar and Rath [2] who had been painstakingly assessing the extent of poverty in India, used calorie levels as an index not just of malnutrition but of pauperisation. Despite near self-sufficiency in food production 20 percent of the population at the base of the pyramid who spend 85 percent of their income on food are unable to consume more than 1,500 calories a day, as against a minimum of 2,300 prescribed by the Planning Commission for rural areas.

None of the above definitions of development is adequate by itself. Raymond Aron for instance emphasises economic growth. Development does not mean only economic growth. Secondly, he says development is the contrast between rich and poor countries. It can be a contrast within the country itself. In Indian context, the concept of two India's "Bharat" and "India" is prevalent and bridging 'dualistic' gaps is cause for a concern. Further, each country is unique in terms of its cultural, social and historical fabric – and this gives rise to a unique set of problems for each country. Thus, it can, in no way, be justified to claim that a country such as Bangladesh must traverse the same path as did the United Kingdom in its endeavour to development.

Neither is Sanjay Lall's allegation that – "high gross national product will imply rapid consumption and hence high social welfare" is too convincing. A high production performance is in no way, automatically indicative of enhanced social welfare. The composition of the goods produced is crucial. It is necessary to see whether or not production is in line with the greater needs of the greater numbers viz. the needy and deprived within a country. Thus the huge 'oil fed" national product figures of the Middle East have in no way contributed positively to the development of crucial indicators such as infant mortality rate, literacy etc. in these countries.

Amulya Kumar's emphasis on "energy consumed per person" rather than per capita income is certainly a move in the right direction, for a minimum per capita income level in no way automatically ensures accessibility to a minimum required food basket. Based on this approach many attempts have been made to define a calorific norm. However, such measurements remain hounded by many problems. Other components of nutrition too are beneficial for human subsistence. Calorific intakes well below the prescribed norm may be, however, compensated by the intakes of such other nutrients. Consequently, some other statisticians have reverted to anthropological measures, such as "height for age", "weight for height" etc. But comparisons across countries using such measures have been found to be meaningful only for a limited age group.

After analysing the above definitions of development one can agree with the following connotations. Development is about improving the well being of people. Raising living standards and improving education, health and equality of opportunity are all essential components of economic development. Ensuring political and civil rights is a broader development goal. Economic growth is an essential means for enabling development, but in itself it is a highly imperfect proxy for progress.

In other words, development is no longer seen as merely an economic goal but as a multi-dimensional concept encompassing economic, as well as political, social and cultural aspects of life.

In the final analysis development involves enhancing social welfare, given the social objectives of a society. Adam Smith had in his 'Wealth of Nations' put forward a proposal which finds popular support even today. His proposal was that so long as each agent in the economy pursues his own self-interest (that is it maximises his own utility) in an uninterrupted fashion, the welfare of the nation is automatically enhanced. This proposal, however, would hold true only under a very stringent set of preconditions, namely, the absence of any 'externalities'.

Externalities arise when one agent's utility – maximising behaviour impinges upon the utility of another. In such a case, the social and private costs of the agents activities differ. This can be illustrated by a taking up the example of setting up of factory. While the private cost is composed of the cost of fixed and variable factors only the social cost (being inclusive of the effects of pollution) is much higher. Being a hindrance to the ecological balance pollution is indeed a concern of the society as a whole, while it is of no direct concern to the factory owner as an individual. In many such instances where the social cost is considerably higher than the private cost, the environment may be an indirect victim.

2.2 Scope of Environmental Protection

Today, no discussion in the field of science, society, planning, policy and politics is complete without a reference to the environment. People from diverse social backgrounds and varied points of view have their own interpretations of the term 'environment'. As such, at the outset of a work devoted to environmental issues, it is necessary to lay down one's definition of the term.

Environment is not only about the birds and the bees, the white tigers, leopards, the rhinos of kaziranga, the export of frog's legs, the use of monkeys for medical experiments or the poaching of elephants for tusks. The environmental issue is one of livelihood and societal relations. It is an issue of the distribution and exploitation of natural resources, the amassing of which results in wealth and the denial of which creates 'the wretched of the earth'. The way the environment is used is also important. It is over exploitation to the extent that natural resources loses its regenerative capacity and is thus a denial to the future generations. As such, the environmental issue is not only one of cross-sectional inequality at a point of time but one of inter-temporal, inter-generational considerations.

Concern for environmental conservation is an ancient phenomenon. Plato attributed the decline in the fertility of soil in ancient Greece to deforestation and subsequent soil erosion and loss of water retaining capacity of the soil. [3] One of the first wild life sanctuaries was near Nineveh [4] signifying the importance of animal conservation and its need for the life of human beings. St. Francis was the first Jesuit preacher to give importance to conservation. Sher Shah Suri, in medieval India, called for effective land management and demarcated 33 percent of the land for forestry purposes. Lewis Mumford [5] has written about the pollution problem in medieval Rome, as being mainly due to firewood smoke and faulty garbage disposal mechanisms. In fact even in modern times, many of the ideas of forest conservation emerged from the writings of Evelyn [6] and Colbert [7] in seventeenth century Europe.

In the nineteenth century the Marxists stressed the man-nature relationship. Friedrich Engles was deeply moved by the pollution problem faced by the working class in England. [8] Engles also explicitly pointed out that man's efforts to conquer nature might pose a threat to material advance. He advocated responsibility towards nature:

Let us not, however, flatter ourselves over much on account of our human victories over nature. For each such victory nature takes its revenge on us. Each victory, it is true, in the first place brings about the results we expected, but in the second and third places it has quite different unforeseen effects which only too often cancel the first. [9]

Karl Marx, reacted sharply to the Russian government's enactments directed against the local inhabitants, which were biased towards the industrial sector. This was in the 1820s. [10] In fact, as Marx was to write later, resistance against this legislation gave an impetus to his thoughts, "the proceedings of the Rhenish Parliament on theft of words provided one of the first occasions for occupying myself with economic questions." [11]

The Marxist tradition of political economy considered the exploitation of natural resources from the colonies. The writings of V.I. Lenin [12] and Rosa Luxemburg [13] highlighted the control and use of natural resources by one class at the expense of another. Though Marxism gave the necessary insight into environment, the subsequent Marxist thinkers just like other philosophers, did not give the environmental issue much importance. A probable reason for this was that resources were being imported into 'metropolis' from the colonies and neo-colonies. The full ecological implications of their exploitation could not be grasped by these thinkers residing in the 'metropolis', however, the concern with environment was patent in Marxism. "Those who insist that such process (environmental one) has nothing to do with Marxism merely ensure that what they choose to call Marxism will have nothing to do with what happens in the world." [14]

2.3 Pollution and Technological Advancement

In the twentieth century, the concern with environmental issues has grown considerably. This is reflected in the emergence of an impressive range of literature on the subject that present a spectrum of views on the environmental problem. Let us examine the recent spurt of literature on environment, which tries to locate the key to the resolution of the ecological problem.

The proponents of the Club of Rome founded by A. Peccei [15] an Italian economist and businessman, to look into the problems related to man and societal interaction are D. Meadows and team [16], Barry Commoner [17], J. Forester [18] and Herman R. Daly. [19]

The basic points arising out of their thesis are (a) that the threat facing humanity arises from exhaustion of natural resources, (b) that the increase of industrial production inevitably leads to pollution and (c) that growth in population increases pressure on resources. This school calls for a halt to industrialisation and consumerism, which are regarded as wasteful. To them, mankind should retard its wheels of progress and go back to nature or else perish along with the planet. Barry Commoner writes:

> Human beings have broken
> Out of the circle of life,
> driven not by biological need,
> but by the social organisation
> which they have devised to
> 'Conquer' nature: means of gaining
> wealth which conflict with those
> which given nature. [20]

According to them, unless we respect these ultimate limits, the planet will perish. A similar view calls for the protection of wild life and trees on grounds of human sensitivity and right to life to all living beings.

Prominent environmental thinking in India is carried on similar lines by people who adhere to what can be called neo-Gandhian thought. Gandhian writings on small-scale industry, self-sufficiency, anti-industrialisation and revival of 'glorious' ancient cultures have been widely read as answers to the ecological crisis.

The second argument within the neo-classical economic framework is that pollution is basically a technological problem and can be overcome easily. [21] Its advocates suggest establishing norms of air and water pollution and taxing the pollution units. Population control is one of the major issues they want tackled in dealing with the environment. Population growth increases the demand for goods and services, and if practices remain unchanged, it implies increased environmental damage. Population growth also increases the need for employment and livelihoods, which-especially in crowded rural areas-exerts additional direct pressure on natural resources. More people also produce more wastes, threatening local health conditions and implying additional stress on the earth's assimilative capacity.

They point out that the environmental issue is a trans class one and it affects everyone irrespective of colour or sex or relation to the production process. They cite cases like Bhopal and Chernobyl disasters to strengthen their point.

The third school believes that the solution to the ecological problem lies in a social reconstruction on the principles of collectivism and planned development under a socialist economy, which takes into account the crucial importance of a radical interaction with nature. It seeks a synthesis between environmentalism and the political economy of development.

2.4 Unequal Development

The world environmental crisis can be classified between the South and the North. There is a basic historical distinction between the two. The environmental crisis in the North is the result of more than 200 years of development through industrial transformation, whereas the crisis in the South is the product of more than 200 years of underdevelopment and inadequate development.

According to Biplab Dasgupta, "Environment performs three basic functions in relation to man. First, it provides us with amenities like enjoyable landscapes and facilities for recreation and a variety of living beings of every colour and shape which makes human life so qualitatively rich. Secondly, environment is a source of natural resources – agricultural, mineral, forestry – which are used in human consumption directly or indirectly. Thirdly, environment acts as a 'sink' for assimilating wastes produced by human civilization; these range from carcases to garbage and carbon-dioxide emitted by the respiration process. [22]

Environment is affected by human beings in four ways. First, 'eutrophic' – the task of decomposing human body and wastes produced in the production and consumption process. Second, 'exploitative'-cropping of plants extraction of minerals, hunting of animals. It is important to note here that the rate of exploitation does not exceed nature's capacity to reproduce. Third, 'disruptive' which are the physical changes brought about by such activities like forest clearance construction of a highway or the setting up of a new township. And fourth, 'chemical and industrial' stress which mainly results from technological development – heavy construction of lead, mercury or radio – active substance. [23]

The human and natural eco-systems are undoubtedly similar in many respects but they are not fully comparable. While the plants and animals adapt themselves to the environment, man/woman distinguishes himself/herself by his/her endeavour to change the environment to suit his/her needs.

Traditional neo-classical economics treat environment in two ways : one approach is to view it as an 'externality' with either positive or negative impact on the cost of operation of an individual firm. A second approach is to treat environment as a commodity for which, like any other commodity, the consumer is expected to pay a price. This approach is justified on the ground that the maintenance of a given environmental standard will require diversion of resources and services from other activities – the 'opportunity cost' of environment.

2.5 New Idea: The Movement

A dissatisfaction came in the late sixties and early seventies with this marginalist approach. This led to the emergence of the environmentalist lobby. This lobby is mainly inspired by two distinct sources : the economists who were disillusioned with the GNP approach towards development, and the ecologists who were alarmed by increasing pollution and rapid depletion of scarce resources. The GNP approach was opposed by structuralist school on both quantitative and qualitative grounds. Another line of argument against GNP was its neglect (being an average) of the distribution of GNP over regions, racial groups and socio-economic classes. They felt that a growth process that benefited a small, wealthy minority and widened the gap between the rich and the poor, could not be equated with development.

The 'environment lobby' was inspired by the ecologists of various description. They shared the structuralist economist's view about the inadequacy of GNP oriented development goals and the need for a qualitative definition of development which would include environment. But where the structuralists were primarily concerned with "social environment'" the ecologists" primary interest was in the physical environment''. Further, while the former viewed environment mainly as an objective of development, the latter viewed environment mainly as a constraint on development.

After 1973 and the oil crisis, the issue of environment got more prominence. A number of international documents attempted to examine environmental problems in the less developed countries in the broader context of international economic relations. [24]

The existing international relations have raised two kinds of issues from the point of view of the debate on environment. First, is the extent to which the rich countries, through their superior purchasing power and control over resources, has succeeded in consuming an overwhelmingly large proportion of the aggregate production of natural resources.

Secondly, it is the extent to which the developed countries control institutions of international trade and have used them to keep the price of resources purchased from the third world countries at a very low level.

The political economy approach locates economic analysis within specific social formation and explains development processes in terms of the benefits and costs they carry for different social classes. It believes that there is no contradiction between man's mastery of nature and his ability to exploit science for his own ends. From a historical materialist perspective, it was society, not science, which placed restrictions on human potential. Lenin elaborated on this view in his discussion of the relationship between man and nature. Man is a product of nature but also a part of nature.

Natural resources facilitated economic growth in the development of the industrialised societies. But the unique contribution of capitalism lay in the way labour was employed in extended reproduction. Redclift opines that "environmental consciousness was itself an important element in the ideological superstructure of modern society and, as such, capable of influencing the pursuit of economic growth". [25] He further argued that the role of science and technology in development was more problematic than what Marx and the early Marxists envisaged. Underdevelopment can no longer be represented largely in terms of the way labour is exploited in dependent capitalist countries.

Ecological degradation in the south assumes emergency proportions largely through the mindless commitment to the economic growth strategy endemic to developed capitalism. The costs of development are expressed not only in terms of class conflict and economic exploitation, but also in the reduction of the natural resource base on which the poor depend for their livelihoods.

The gap that exists between our understanding of environmental change in developing countries, and holistic development theory, is matched by an equally important gulf between the identification of environmental problems and the implementation of workable policies to ensure their solution. Present development policy seriously exacerbates the environmental problems that accompany resource depletion in the developing countries. Choices in development models exist which would permit a sustainable development, but they are not widely canvassed in the industrialised countries and would necessitate some uncomfortable changes in expectations and demand. 'Development' is sustained by economic ideology rather than resources.

According to Redclift there are four ways in which societies are prevented from elaborating effective environmental policies through the mystification of environmental values. [26]

'High technology' and the international division of labour give us a platform to ignore the links between the 'causes' and 'effects' of resource depletion. This it does by the priority it gives to our own physiological and psychological needs.

Secondly, the source of mystification is 'externalities ' that is the environmental costs that are not included in the market price of a commodity or service. The methodologies of environmental societies have been predicted upon the need to measure and quantify these 'externalities' more rigorously.

Thirdly, resource misuse or depletion involves questions of intergenerational equity which are rarely, if ever, considered in policy discussions. In most societies future benefits and costs of protecting the environment are values that are less relative (that is they are discounted), to current benefits and costs.

Finally, our ability to respond effectively to the environmental consequences of resource use is seriously impaired by each society's commitment to its own ideology of economic growth.

Economic relations between developed and developing countries contribute to environmental problems in a number of ways. First, each individual in an industrial society makes larger demands on the world's resources than does each individual in the less developed countries. It is intellectually dishonest to attribute the global resource crisis to the population explosion in the less developed countries. Second, the satisfaction of our own economic demands in the industrialised countries can not be met only from our own resource base. To a great extent, the resource and environmental pressures felt in the south are linked to high living standards and wasteful resource use in the north. Third, industrial societies are notorious in not being able to recycle discarded waste, with consequences that are both environmentally and socially damaging.

Thus our perceptions of the environment have evolved with the development process. Environmentalism is an elusive concept which has produced complex and different social movements. The view that nature exists for human being is uncompromisingly challenged. Nature needs to be protected for its own sake, not merely to preserve its potential for human being. This concern with the stewardship of the natural environment has been taken from the idea that human respect for nature is lost in the pursuit of material gain.

One of radical environmentalism's principal weaknesses is the absence of a theory which explains how the new society is to be brought about. In the interim, the heightened environmental consciousness dictates a search for less wasteful ways of using natural resources and a return to human scale technologies.

Sandbach distinguishes two types of environmentalism, one that is basically ecological and scientific and the other that is more radical in inspiration. The second type of environmentalism is more anti-establishment, less concerned with environmental systems, but more with whether or not science and technology are compatible with humanistic principles.

2.6 Environment and Development

Environmental problems are basically developmental problems. In the developed countries the lower priority needs such as freedom from pollution or planning assume importance because higher priority needs such as housing and food have already been satisfied for majority groups. Indeed, the extent to which high priority needs are satisfied seriously prejudices the satisfaction of low priority needs. By contrast, in developing countries the higher priority needs retain their priority and constitute the battle ground for environmental politics.

The basic difference in the approach was summed up like this at founex : In mid – 1971, a group of experts were invited by the secretary general of the United Nations Conference on Human Environment, to spend a few days together in a motel in Founex, a village on the outskirts of Geneva. The experts were from many countries and disciplines, and held diverse political - social views. They were of the opinion that in industrialised countries, it is appropriate to view development as the cause of environmental problems; in developing countries, development becomes essentially a cure for their environmental problems, of which the most pressing is poverty itself. At the same time, however, it was recognised that while poor countries face environmental problems because of the lack of development, the very process of development also gives rise to such problems.

The Founex Report recognised that the roots of most current environmental problems could be traced to the activities of industrialised countries but they were of equal concern to the third world for three reasons. First, many of these problems extend beyond national boundaries and threaten the entire world's population. Second, some problems are common to both types of countries – the urban crisis for example. Further, third world countries had to learn from the mistakes and distortions that had characterised the development of the industrialised countries. 'Social' or 'human' environment thus emerged as an important area of concern. This demonstrated to the third world the relevance of environmental issues, assured them that they were in no way conflicting with the present or future development potential of a country and that it did not serve only the interests of a rich minority.

Environmental degradation invariably results in increased economic inequalities in which the poor suffer the most. Environmental degradation and social injustice are two sides of the same coin. The human condition and the state of the environment are closely related to each other.

Environment and development are not opposing but complementary to each other. 'Careless technology'- in the shape of big dams, for instance-neither improves the environment nor amounts to development. The most overwhelming immediate lesson of course, is the total lack of any coherent policy on such issues, despite the headstart provided to any environmental planning process.

According to Satish Saberwal, "The social crisis in India is not specific, local and temporary; it is general, widespread and persistent. It is evident even in all branches of government: political parties, legislatures, bureaucracy, judiciary, in key societal institutions like the universities and trade unions." [27] Because of this social crisis, different kinds of social movements are taking place. "These social movements simultaneously work at two levels. At one they are defensive, seeking to protect civil society from the tentacles of the centralising state; at another, they are assertive seeking to change civil society from within and in the process putting forward a conception of the good life". [28]

At the level of the economy, they have brought to the fore, conflicts over productive resources that were hitherto neglected or peripheral to the concerns of political organisations. The scene of the 'traditional' class struggle was the field and factory. The ecology movement represents a new kind of class struggle over natural resources like forests and water.

On the political plane these environmental movements are distinctive in so far as they operate almost wholly outside the traditional party system. Indeed, much of the membership and force of contemporary social movements (world wide) is the reflection of people's disappointment and frustration with – and their search for alternatives to – the political process, political parties, the state and the capture of state power.

These movements have not arisen in a vacuum. It is surely no accident that the latter half of the 20th century has seen the emergence of such movements in the first, second and third worlds. In the third world modernisation on the western model, once so attractive to nationalist elites, has failed to realise its expectations.

The present pattern of economic development is depleting our stock of soil, water and plant resources at a terrifying rate. This process is causing tremendous deprivation to millions of people in the countryside – people who depend on these resources for subsistence. The most critically affected sections of society are the poor and landless peasants, women and tribals. It is a question of sheer survival and not of enhancing the quality of life.

The Indian ecological/green movements can be termed 'new'. It is because they respond to social needs which have been more recently generated by development. Environmental degradation as a threat to livelihood and welfare is the product of recent industrial development.

These movements generate and wield social power through the social mobilisation of their participants. This social power is at once generated by and derived from the social movement itself rather than from any institution, political or otherwise. In fact, institutionalisation weakens social movements and state political power negates or neutralises them. Social movements require flexible, adaptive and non-authoritarian organisation to direct social power in pursuit of social goals.

These social movements are cyclical in two senses. First, they respond to circumstances, which change as a result of political, economic and perhaps ideological fluctuations or cycles.

Secondly, social movements tend to have life-cycles of their own. Social movements, their membership, mobilisation and strength, tend to be cyclical because the movements mobilise people in response to circumstances, which are themselves cyclical.

The social movements in the western countries are middle class based. This class composition of the social movements, of course, reflects the changing stratification of western society. In the third world countries, social movements are predominantly workers based. Most of its members are victims of social injustice and deprivation. These third world social movements are at once cooperative, competitive or conflictive.

These popular social movements and organisations are instruments of people's struggle against exploitation, oppression, and for survival and identity in a complex dependent society. In the third world countries stratification based on region, occupation, race, colour, ethnicity, language, religion etc. are elements in, and instruments of domination and liberation.

However, there are significant areas of conflict and competition among social movements. Movements of different religions and ethnicities, races etc. compete and conflict with each other.

2.7 Conclusion

Thus the above analysis discusses different interpretations of development According to Raymond Aron development is economic growth. Mahabubul Haq also has the same opinion. He says development goals should be elimination of malnutrition, disease, illiteracy, squalor, unemployment and inequality. Amulya Kumar Reddy has a different opinion. In his scheme of things, is the index how much energy a person consumes, rather than his per capita income, this comprises both calories in the shape of food and other external forms like fuel for cooking and lighting. Economists like Dandekar and N. Rath see development in terms of used calorie levels as an index. But all the above interpretations are incomplete. Development is no longer seen as merely an economic goal but as a multi- dimensional concept encompassing economic, as well as political, social and cultural aspects of life.

The concept of environment has also been defined. How environment has been seen in different times by different schools of thought Gandhian writings on small-scale industry, self-sufficiency, anti-industrialisation and revival of glorious ancient cultures have been widely read as answers to the ecological crisis. Another school believes in population control as the answer for environmental problems. The third school believes that the solution to the ecological problem lies in a social reconstruction on the principles of collectivism and planned development under a socialist economy, which takes into account the crucial importance of a radical interaction with nature. It seeks a synthesis between environmentalism and the political economy of development.

It is also crystal clear that social movements are important agents of social transformation and new vision, despite their defensiveness, limitations and relations to the state. Social movements are also important because they fill the void which the state and other social and cultural institutions are unable or reluctant to act and fill in the interests of their members.

Notes

1. Darry! D'Monte, *Temples or Tombs: Industry Versus Environment–Three Controversies*, Centre for Science and Environment, 1985, New Delhi.

2. V. M. Dandekar and N. Rath, Poverty in India, *Economic and Political Weekly*, January 1971.

3. As quoted in R.F. Dasmann, *Planet in Peril*, Penguin, 1972, p. 99.

4. *Ibid.*

5. Lewis Mumford, *The City of History*, Penguin, 1966.

6. John Evelyn, *Silva – A Discourse on Forest Trees*, 1664.

7. Colbert, *French Forest Ordinance of 1669.*

8. Friedrich Engles, *The Condition of the Working Class*, Blackwell, 1958.

9. Friedrich Engles, *Dialectics of Nature*, Progress Publishers, 1934.

10. Karl Marx, *The Critique of Political Economy*, Franz Dunker, 1859.

11. Karl Marx and Friedrich Engles, *Rheinische Zeitung 1813-1814*, werke, 1956.

12. V.I. Lenin, *Imperialism: the Highest Stage of Capitalism*, Progress Publications, 1978.

13 Rosa Luxemburg, *The Accumulation of Capital*, New Haven, Yale University Press, 1951.

14. A. Faster – Carter, "Neo Marxist Analysis to Development and Underdevelopment" in E.de Kadt and G. Williams (eds.) *Sociology and Development*, Tavistock, 1974.

15. A. Peccei, *Where are We? Where are We Living*? Sucesso, 1971, and A. Peccei, *The Predicament of Mankind*, Sucesso, 1970.

16. D.H. Meadows, et al., *The Limits of Growth*, New York, Universe Books, 1972.

17. Barry Commoner, *Encirclement*, Paris, Sevil, 1972 (The closing circel in English).

18. J. Forester, *World Dynamics*, Allen Press, 1971.

19. Herman R. Daly, *Towards a Steady-State Economy*, W.H. Freeman, 1973.

20. Barry Commoner, No. 17

21. Fredrick R. Anderson, *Environmental Improvement through Economic Incentives* John Hopkins University Press, Baltimore.

22. Biplab Dasgupta, The Environment Debate: Some Issues and Trends, *Economic and Political Weekly*, Annual 1978, P-385.

23. *Ibid.*

24. *Ibid.*

25. Redclift Michael, *Development and the Environmental Crisis Red or Green Alternatives*? Methuen and Co. 1984.

26. Ibid.

27. Satish Saberwal, the Problem, *Seminar*, New Delhi, July 1987.

28. Ramchandra Guha, The Problem, *Seminar*, New Delhi, March 1989.

3

Ganga Mukti Andolan

Indian development process which has been adopted after independence has made India a self-reliant, relatively developed and modern country but at the same time this development model has caused tremendous environmental degradation and problems. This environmental degradation has mainly affected the lives of the poor, women and tribals. Their lives and lifestyles have been changing according to the environmental change. The fisherfolk of Bihar is an example of the development model leading to acute environmental degradation.

After independence the policy makers in India were enthusiastic enough to make India a leading industrialised nation, but they paid little attention to environmental degradation and pollution caused by it. Industrial hazards have been affecting health and survival of the people. In addition, this industrial development also leads to polluting natural resources like water, air, land etc.

The decade of seventies has a landmark place in the politics and society of India. Those were the days of euphoria. The trauma of the failed Naxalite uprising had not been forgotten and the Nav Nirman Andolan and, later, the Jay Prakash Narayan led Sampoorna Kranti Andolan had shaken up the Indian society and polity.

The seventies also witnessed the emergence of social movements involving peasants fighting against bonded labour and for forest rights. The Chipko movement, Shramik Sangathan and Bhoomi Seva movement of Maharashtra are the best examples. These were social movements that centred around the needs of the people. Along with Narmada Bachao Andolan a new environmental upsurge began. It was marked by other movements such as Koel Karo Struggle, Chhattisgarh Mukti Morcha, Ganga Mukti Andolan and many others.

The Ganga Mukti Andolan was started by the fisherfolk of the Ganges region of Bhagalpur district in Bihar. They were suffering from two types of problems. One was the feudal "Panidari" system which had been prevailing in this region since long time and the other was the industrial pollution in the Ganges river which was a capitalist problem. Both were exploitative and constituted a threat to the survival of the fisherfolk. Against this, fisherfolk launched a movement that came to be known as Ganga Mukti Andolan (G.M.A.)

3.1 Origin and Factors of the Movement

The Ganges passes through the northern part of the district. It touches the district at Tulsipur, forming the boundary with Parbatta block of Munger district for about ten miles. It enters the district opposite Sultanganj. The Ganges then flows northwards to Bhagalpur where it takes a bend to the South to Kahalgaon. From here the river flows eastward for eight miles up to Patharghatta where it is joined by the Kosi. The river is navigable throughout the year by all types of boats.

3.2 Panidari: The Feudal Aspect

The fishing communities were exploited by 'Waterlords' or 'Panidars' (who controls the water) who extracted heavy taxes for the right to fish in the Ganges. Some eighty kilometers from Sultanganj to Peerpanti of the Ganga river had been under the possession for generations of two Panidar families who claimed hereditary ownership or Panidari over this part of the river. The Ganges and its associate rivers like – Burhi Gandak, Kosi and Sone also came under the Panidari System. The area of the Ganges was prone to both flood and drought. Interestingly, there was a shortage of water for irrigation in this area despite its proximity to the river.

The inhabitants of this area are mainly *Gangota, Machuara, Dhanuk, Gwala, Tanti, Bhumihar and Rajput* castes. This area is dominated by middle castes and backward castes. This is also mentioned in one of the famous books of P. C. Roychaudhary's Bihar District Gazetteers (1962).

Panidari in the Ganges was controlled by two families that secured it in the Mughal Era. It is believed that the Mughal Emperor Akbar honoured one of his Kanoongoes [1] Pareshnath Ghosh with the title of Mahashyajee (Synonym for Sir in English) and rewarded him with Panidari rights of the Ganges from Sultanganj to Peerpanti. The Western portion covers the area from Barari to Sultanganj. It was called 'Chanan Jalkar Zamindari [2] and was controlled by Mahashya Mahesh Ghosh and his family. The eastern portion consists from Barari to Peerpanti. It comes under 'Muksaspur Jalkar Zamindari', the control of which was divided between Mahashaya Mahesh Ghosh and Musharaf Hussain Parmanik. Mahashaya Mahesh Ghosh had given half of his Zamindari to one of his chief servants Mohammed Ghani Khan. Interestingly, this Panidari right is hegemonised in the name of God almighty. Prominent Gods and Goddesses under whose names Panidari was entitled were (a) Sri Sri Bhairab Nath jee, (b) Sri Sri Thakur Basudev Roy, (c) Sri Sri Shivajee [3] etc. It was done in the name of Gods because of the fear of outsiders who started capturing lands in this region during 1930s.

Right from the days of Emperor Akbar Panidari was free from state revenue. It was continued during the British period also. The Governor General in Council, by Article 1973 (Revenue) in 1908 and 1910, issued an order and declared 80 kilometers of the Ganges area revenue free.

In independent India there was an effort by the state to abolish the Panidari system in 1961. The then Deputy Collector of Bhagalpur district tried to abolish it. In May 1961, Panidars appealed to the Patna High Court and got a 'stay order' in August 1961. In 1964 the High Court delivered its judgement in favour of the Panidars. In its judgement, the High Court had declared that this fishing right had been given by a Mughal Emperor and had been continuing ever since. It also stated that Panidari was different from Zamindari as it did not involve an immovable property like land. As such it did not come under the jurisdiction of the Bihar Land Reforms Act 1950. In 1972, the Bihar government instead of passing another legislation, preferred to file a writ in the Supreme court against this judgement. The Supreme court had however, for some reason made only one Panidar a party to the appeal.

3.3 Working of Panidari

Panidari had a well-planned machinery. Panidars sub-let their Panidari rights to contractors. The contractors gave it further on lease to the fisherfolk. Through this mechanism the Panidars levied taxes on over forty thousand fishermen living in subsistence levels in nearly sixty riverine villages of the Bhagalpur district. The tax amount for fish varied according to the size of boats, nets and different seasons. This lease was for nine months only and fisherfolk opting for the rainy season had to pay extra. Generally the income accrued through such taxes to these waterlords amounted to somewhere between rupees thirty to forty million per annum. [4] If members of the fishing community were unable to pay the levy, they were prevented from fishing. Attempts at opposition were greeted with the capture of boats and nets. The levy amount was collected through anti social elements at gun-point.

The major threat for the fisherfolk was from the groups of criminals active in this region. These criminals usually used to snatch their expensive nets, boats and other belongings. Some of the criminals regularly collected money by their muscle power. Literally, the Ganges was in captivity. On the one hand, *Ghatdars* [5] had controlled it and on the other hand it was in the clutches of Panidars. The system of Panidari and contractorship were persisting along the Ganges.

The fisherfolk also find it difficult to arrange the loans. Usually, the fisherfolk were not able to get loans from the nationalised banks for buying nets and boats. So they had to go to the landlords and moneylenders who charged high rate of interest. They charge high rate of interest from fisherfolk. There were cooperative committees for the fisherfolk but they helped only the few influential ones among them. These reasons compelled a few fisherfolk to give up this occupation and migrate. [6]

In Bihar the fishery and related activities are conducted by the government. The Bihar state government collects tax in the Ganges region through contractors or fisherfolk cooperative society. It collects annually about ten lakh rupees as tax. However, the office-bearers of these cooperatives and the contractors manage to collect more than ten crore rupees. [7] The cooperative societies for fisherfolk neither represent their problems nor work for their welfare. Rather it is an organisation which directly or indirectly works under the clutches of bureaucrats and politicians and is exploiting the fisherfolk. The officers of cooperative societies and contractors also use criminals and anti – social elements for collecting money and giving leases. Usually the office-bearers of cooperatives are either nominees of the local MLAs (Member of Legislative Assembly) or people of influence.

Another situation which was hindering the prosperity of fisherfolk was the problem of cloth net, fish egg and chipping. Seventy percent of existing chipping available in India come from the river Ganges. The eggs and chippings were available at nineteen places in the Ganges in Bihar (Koilabar, Kurjee, Bansghat, Fatuha, Bakhtiarpur, Mokama, Munger, Sultanganj, Bhagalpur, Kahalgaon, Kursela, Kathagola, Manihari, Sahebganj etc. in Bihar and in Bengal at Sakari gali, Maharajpur, Rajmahal, Manikchak ghat and Farakka). In the process of picking up eggs and chippings, ninety percent of fish were destroyed. This was also one of the reasons for the shortage of fish in the Ganges. The use of cloth net for picking up fish was very dangerous. By this process fish in their early age and their food moss were destroyed. Moss cleans the water of the Ganges. The use of cloth net for picking up fish is strictly banned in other states but it is being openly practiced in Bihar.

3.4 Industrial Pollution and its Impact

The problems confronting fishing communities were multidimensional. They not only faced major constraints to their development as a result of the feudal nature of the Panidari system, but also due to the fact that an increasing amount of industrial effluent without proper treatment was being channelled into the Ganges river, rapidly depleting fish stocks. The Ganges water was getting more and more polluted day by day due to garbage, excreta from both countryside and urban areas and due to factory wastes. In this polluted water fish, eggs and chippings were not growing properly.

A report prepared by K. S. Belgrami and J. S. Dutta Munshi of Bhagalpur University [8] confirmed that around one hundred and twelve kilometers of the Ganges from Barauni to Bhagalpur was heavily polluted. Industrial wastes were dumped into the river by a shoe factory owned by the Bata Company situated at Mokama, a McDowells distillery at Kanpur, an oil refinery at Barauni, a thermal power station at Kahalgaon and a fertiliser factory located upstream from Bhagalpur. Fish survived for only forty eight hours in the water at the point where the Bata shoe factory dumped its wastes and for only five hours at the McDowell distillery's mixing zone. The quantity and flammable nature of the wastes discharged from the oil refinery near Munger is so large that in 1968 the Ganges was reported to have caught fire. The polluted zone at Barauni acted as a barrier to the upstream movement of fish and affected their spawning. The township of Bhagalpur and nearby industries also contributed to the pollution due to the domestic sewage industrial effluents and the run off fertilisers and pesticides from agricultural fields. This had drastically reduced the amount of fish caught and the subsequent deterioration in the economic position of the fishing community. The residuals from the industries of Mokama-Barauni area and the polluted water of the Ganges made the land sterile and agriculturally unproductive.

The following table [9] shows the clear picture of residuals from the factories.

Measurement	Bata Shoe Factory	McDowell Distillery
Colour	Black / Brown	Black / Brown
Temperature (C)	18 – 35	42 – 45
Dirt (N. T. U)	310 – 490	340 – 550
Hydrogen Aayon (P.H) [10]	6.9 – 8.6	4.9 – 6.6
Dilute Oxygen (P.P.M) [11]	0 – 2.4	0 – 1.6
Potasium (P.P.M)	140.8 – 151.6	41.3 – 40.4
Sodium (P.P.M)	74.9 – 82.4	120.6 – 139.2

This table demonstrates that industrial residuals from Bata factory and McDowell had polluted the Ganges water. At certain points the water has become coloured. The pollution of water was about ten times higher than the normal water. The temperature of the water was very high due to residuals from the McDowell factory. This pollution had badly affected the level of diluted oxygen.

The fisherfolk of Kahalgaon were aware of the happenings at the D.C.M. factory at Kota in Rajasthan, the poisonous water of Kanpur due to McDowell distillery and Bata shoe factory of Mokama. They were also aware of the reasons which made the water of Damodar river black. The water of north Bihar had become yellow because of garbage from sugar mills. This problem had multi-dimensional effects. First the fish of the river were causing health problems among the people because it was taking dirt from the river. Second, there was a shortfall of fish in the region resulting in impoverishment of fisherfolk. Third, the protein content in the diet of the people was reducing. In addition to industrial effluents there were many poisonous chemicals like DDT, BHC, dieldrin and aldrin which were used very frequently for agricultural crops, also proved dangerous for fish. According to a study, there was a maximum concentration of DDT at

Haridwar followed by, at Patna and Farakka. While at Haridwar, it was 3,700 nanogram per gram, in Patna it was 1,300 and at Farakka 1,100. Similarly, the concentration of almost all polychlorinated biphenyl congeners and organochlorine pesticides was much higher in these places. While it was 270 nanogram per gram at Kanpur, it was 220 at Patna and 200 at Haridwar. These chemicals, which were biologically non-degradable compounds, came into the river as agriculture and health drive run-offs and the concentration was much higher than the permissible limit. These get accumulated in the body and can lead to serious ailments like cancer or adversely affect the kidneys and brains of those who consume the river fish regularly. [12]

S. N. Mukherjee, Biplab Mitra and S. K. Majumdar of Central Fuel Research Institute had conducted a study on the probable pollution effects of the thermal power station. According to their study the flyash content in the Raj Mahal coal field is 48 percent. [13] When this coal is used in Kahalgaon super thermal power project, it has severe pollution effects. They also possess hot sulphur which reacts with oxygen in the air and makes sulphur dioxide. Sulphur dioxide again reacts with the atmosphere's moisture and converts into Sulphuric acid.

The then chairman of the Central Pollution Control Board Dr. Nilay Choudhary had also accepted in 1984 that there was no pollution control system in thirty one out of forty eight thermal power station. [14] There was pollution control system only in seventeen stations out of which six were functioning properly.

A small thermal power station of Gomia had destroyed the paddy crops of five kilometers around the area. [15] It was very difficult to imagine the devastation that was caused by the Kahalgaon thermal power station, which was fourteen times smaller than the Bokaro power station. It harms not only crops and plants but human beings also. Different types of new diseases were coming up in this area. At the first stage of establishment of Kahalgaon thermal power station people of fifty five villages (by now many more) had been displaced. Over all, almost one and half lakh people of around twenty thousand families had migrated.

According to United Nations Population Fund, today the Ganges is the most polluted river in the world. [16] The Ganges covers the area of two thousand five hundred twenty five kilometers in which more than one thousand kilometer are polluted. The industrial garbage and urban pollution has turned the Ganges into a huge gutter. According to scientists, if 'Pesial Californ' [17] bacteria is more than five hundred in one hundred cubic meter water then it is dangerous and useless. But surprisingly these bacteria are available more in number in the Ganges river. That is why the Ganges water has been branded into 'E' category at many places and its use is banned because of its pollution and dirtiness.

The Ganges water is pure up to about two hundred and fifty kilometers of its origin near Gangotri but after Rishikesh its water becomes polluted. The main reason behind this is big cities which are situated at the bank of the Ganges like Haridwar, Kannauj, Kanpur, Allahabad, Varanasi, Calcutta and other big cities with heavy industries. There are about one hundred and fifty large scale industries in all these cities in which only twelve industries have the pollution control system. According to a study of Central Water Sewage Control Board about eleven lakh fifty thousand tons of chemical fertilisers and around two thousand five hundred seventy three ton pesticides had been used on the banks of the Ganges in 1977-78 alone. According to an estimate, everyday about 19,65,900 kilogram of polluted residual joins the Ganges of which almost 10,90,900 kilogram joins in Uttar Pradesh and 3,79,000 in West Bengal. In Haridwar, about seventeen lakh fifty thousand litres and in Varanasi around twelve crore litres of polluted water join in the Ganges. It is also polluted due to effluents from Bharat Heavy Electricals Limited and the polluting residuals of Haridwar.

In 1980, a Chemical Fertiliser Factory IFCO started production in Phoolpur near Allahabad. Its estimated production capacity per day was about 1,550 tons of urea. This place, because of the factory and its inhabitants was using about 13,500 cubic meters water everyday and returns around 5,500 cubic meter poisonous water. According to scientists of the Central Island Fisheries Research Institute of Allahabad, huge amount of fish have died and animals have been affected in the area of sixteen kilometers from the place where these residuals join. [18] Another research team of Banaras Hindu University states that the Ganges water is not suitable for drinking near Allahabad, Varanasi and Patna in the rainy season because of its dirtiness. Calcutta is the most polluted and most industrialised city situated on the banks of the Ganges. It has about eighty seven jute mills, seven leather refinery, five paper industries and four wine factories. In addition to this, there are around three hundred sixty one drainage of mud water which continuously join the Ganges.

3.5 Non-industrial Pollutants

Apart from the industrial pollution, there are some non-industrial elements also which are causing pollution in the Ganges. The most common are corpses and the ashes of dead bodies. According to Dr. B. D. Tripathy of Banaras Hindu University, every year around 30,000 half burnt corpses and 200 to 300 tons ashes are thrown into the Ganges at Varanasi. [19] This situation is prevailing all along the bank of the Ganges throughout the year. According to a study, around 6,000 corpses of animals are seen flowing every year at Manikarnika Ghat and Harishchandra Ghat. [20] According to an observation by Central Water Pollution Control Board the Ganges is very clear ten kilometers before Kanpur city but gradually becomes polluted and discoloured till Kishanpur village. [21] It is all because of the garbage and poisonous residuals of Bharonghat pumping station, cloth mills and leather factories situated in Kanpur. In addition to this, dirty water from the Kandensar thermal power station and of J. K. Rayance also joins the Ganges and make it polluted.

A boom in housing along a seven kilometer stretch upstream of the bathing ghats of Varanasi and poor performance of the pumping stations are the main reasons for the persistently high levels of bacteria and bio-oxygen demand (BOD) [22] in the water according to Virbhadra Mishra of the Swachya Ganga Laboratory. [23]

A team of the Uttar Pradesh Jal Nigam which is implementing the Ganga Action Plan (G.A.P.) and the Uttar Pradesh Pollution Control Board (P.C.B.) found the BOD levels to be around 5mg per litre during a monitoring exercise in which samples were taken from the same points in the river. The pollution in the seven kilometer bathing zone in Varanasi is most hazardous as millions of pilgrims take the holy dip only to carry infection to long distances in the country. Ironically, the G.A.P. does not consider bacterial count to be a parameter of cleanliness.

The joint monitoring revealed that the bacterial level (fecal coliform) which should ideally be zero in bathing water, was as high as 10,000 MPN (most probable number per hundred cubic centimeter) down stream of the bathing zone. The bacterial level apparently increases during bathing as it has been found to be less than a tenth upstream of the zone. The project authorities in the Jal Nigam had earlier claimed that the high bacterial levels were caused by the dumping of flowers from thousands of temples in Varanasi. Water samples have also revealed a substantial amount of human and animal excreta, according to Virbhadra Mishra. He has demanded an end to the unplanned growth of housing along the river, interceptors for the drains that pour the polluted water into the river and more treatment plants. He claims that each of the five sewage pumping stations have drainage connected to them. Whenever the pumps malfunction, which is quite often, the untreated material is allowed to be released into the river.

3.6 Role of Farakka Barrage

The fishing community livelihood has also been indirectly affected by the Farakka Barrage of West Bengal. Built to divert water to the Hoogly river, the barrage prevents the migration of fish like the *Jingha* and *Hilsa* to the Himalayan foothills where it breeds thereby contributing to the depletion of fish stock.

Water of many rivers of West Bengal, Bihar, Uttar Pradesh, Madhya Pradesh, Rajasthan and Haryana directly goes in Ganges.

Farakka Barrage has prevented the migration of marine fish in these rivers. There are many fish which inhabit in fresh water, but breed in marine water. Prawn is one such example. Similarly *Hilsa* inhabit in marine water, but breed in fresh icy water.

Due to blockade of their migration routes by Farakka Barrage, breeding process today is seriously hampered. Prior to this barrage, during monsoon, there used to be a very high population of eggs and spawns in this stretch of Ganga. After catering to the local needs a substantial amount of fish and prawns were used to send to other states, but now only about twenty five percent of the local demand is available in this same stretch. According to Uday Kant Chaudhary, then Chairman of Bihar State Fisheries Development Board, Bihar's needs alone are not getting fulfilled.

Farakka Barrage has resulted in the depletion of seventy five percent of fish population of all these rivers. Not only their members have dwindled, but large fishes are no longer spotted. As a result, millions of fishermen have reached a state of destitution. The fisherfolk from Bihar are hence migrating to West Bengal and other neighbouring countries like Bangladesh. The Farakka barrage has adversely affected the ecology and the economy of Bangladesh too.

Deforestation and consequent erosion in the catchment areas of the Ganges combine with big dams construction to increase river siltation leading to recurrent flooding of the river. In ten years in Bhagalpur area alone some thirty to forty meters of the river bank has been swept away, along with houses and many lives. It is said that during the early 1980s the Bihar state government allocated Rs. 400,000 for the construction of an embankment to protect the riverine villages. But the entire amount is said to have been squandered by local politicians and irrigation officials. [24]

3.7 Ganga Mukti Andolan (G.M.A.)

All these feudal and capitalist exploitation of their community made the fisher folk realise the deprivation they are subject to. An accumulated growth of resentment led them to stake their rights.

In a meeting held on 22nd February 1982 in Kagajeetola of Kahalgaon in Bhagalpur district. The fishing community decided to put the issues in the broader perspective so as to involve maximum people. On 18th March 1982 fisherfolk of Kahalgaon took out a procession and placed their demands to the Block Development Officer (B.D.O.). The slogan that sought to abolish taxes on water (Panidari) was for the first time raised in this demonstration. Inspired by the life and work of the prominent Gandhian, Shri Jay Prakash Narayan and the organisation formed by him 'Chhatra Yuva Sangharsh Vahini' (C.Y.S.V.), a conference of fisherfolk took place on 4th April 1982 in which about two hundred men and women of nineteen villages participated. In this conference a people's organisation, 'Jal Shramik Sangh' was constituted. This conference was of historical importance due to many reasons. The social and cultural issues were taken up for the first time only after this conference. In this conference, apart from Panidari, issues of casteism, alcoholism, participation of women and pollution were discussed.

3.8 Formation of G.M.A

As the organisation grew among the fishing communities in the riverine villages of Bhagalpur district, a broad based movement developed, called the Ganga Mukti Andolan (G.M.A.) to tackle the problems related to the fishing communities. The journalists, academicians, theatre persons and cultural activists joined this movement. The pattern of inappropriate development in the region which continued to erode the livelihood of traditional fishing communities came to focus the attention.

In 1984, when Ganga Mukti Andolan (G.M.A.) was fighting against the Panidari system and closure of Kahalgaon Super Thermal Power Station, the most tragic Bhopal gas incident and Chernobyl incident of Russia occurred. Both of these tragedies made the people aware about the after effects of thermal power stations. The G.M.A. strongly advocated to close down the thermal power station. The G.M.A. activists kept themselves busy in making the masses conscious about different environmental tragedies and the harm caused by it. In this context the G.M.A. distributed a pamphlet in Bhagalpur district titled 'Stop Bhagalpur to become Bhopal'. Through this pamphlet G.M.A. raised many broader issues. They demanded ban on the use of pesticides. The debate of indigenous culture versus foreign culture was also discussed and the whole concept of 'Development' was questioned.

With the passage of time the scope of the movement spread and so also the issues raised by it. The G.M.A. brought up many issues before the people. Prominent among them were (a) abolition of Panidari system, (b) abolition of zamindari in ghat area, (c) establishment of pollution control system in every thermal power station, (d) removal of bata factory from this area, (e) closure of the McDowell's wine factory, (f) closure of the fertiliser factory of Barauni, (g) prevention of the use of imported pesticides, (h) making a fish ladder in Farakka Barrage and (i) exemption of the cess of underwater land of flood plain area. It also demanded that the cultivator should be given the ownership of land, that the Ganges should be prevented from being made poisonous and that the flood problem of flood should be solved for ever.

On 4th September 1984 a *'Machhua-Navik Sammelan'* was organised in Kahalgaon. Following this the G.M.A. took up two things very seriously i.e. (a) mass contact and (b) demonstration. In 1987, it organised a huge boat demonstration. This time the movement covered around ninety percent of the people living on the bank of the Ganges in Bihar. The boat demonstration started on 8th April 1987 from Kursela of Katihar district and went via Bateshwarsthan, Kahalgaon, Bhagalpur, Sultanganj, Munger, Ballahpur, Simaria, Banpur Tola, Khusnipur, Fatuha, Gayghat to Patna. On the way to Patna, the movement organised many demonstrations and meetings. On 21st April 1987, the demonstration culminated in a huge public meeting on the bank of the Ganges river near Patna College. When the meeting was going on, the Ganges was crowded with hundreds of boats. The atmosphere was very tense with the feeling of deprivation and it seemed as if a bloody violence was lurking in the horizon. This boat demonstration and the meeting spread the message of the movement throughout Bihar.

After this the G.M.A. demonstrated in Patna city and met the then Chief Minister Bhagwat Jha Azad who promised to abolish Panidari on eighty kilometer of the Ganges. His successor Bindeshwari Dubey had also promised the same. But nothing concrete could come out.

In 1990, the G.M.A. again took up with new enthusiasm and deep concern the socio-economic, political and cultural issues revolving around the fishing community. On 14-15 May, 1990 on the bank of Ganges in Patna Engineering College campus, a state level programme 'JAMGHAT' was organised. Hundreds of people took the oath to fight against any collective or individual injustice to the people. After this decision the fisher's cooperative and Panidars found themselves in a very awkward position and started harassing fisherfolk. They started snatching the boats and nets of fisherfolks. Again on 14th June 1990, the fisherfolk organised a programme 'JUTAN' at Rajghat in Patna against all these misdeeds. In this meeting the fisherfolk reiterated their oath to fight against injustice and repression.

Through their organisational and rigorous campaigning work, the Ganga Mukti Andolan was able to release thirty of the eighty kilometers of the Ganga river from the Panidar's possession. Fishing communities could freely fish in thirty kilometer of the Ganges without paying taxes. In addition, the Andolan had organised campaigns against the pollution of the Ganga and other environmental problems which affected fishing communities, as a way of influencing legislators and policy makers.

3.9 Role of Women in G.M.A.

Women played an important role in this movement in many ways. Firstly, they were very helpful in mobilising the people. Secondly, when this movement campaigned against alcoholism, women forced male members of their families not to touch alcohol. [25] Thirdly, when male activists of this movement were attacked by criminals and goons of Panidars, the women formed a chain surrounding male members and compelled the criminals to leave the place. It was inspired by Chipko movement. Fourthly, when movement was at its peak, some mismanagement of funds were found and women were made incharge of funds. The women thus emerged leaders of the movement. They handled all these responsibilities very successfully. Fifthly, women played a very crucial role in organising the programmes and meetings. They used to sing songs related to the movement and this worked as a catalyst and helped greatly in mobilising the people.

Gradually G.M.A. broadened its issues. The members protested against the influence of western culture on indigenous culture, crime, communalism and chaos in the society. It was not against development, modernisation and progress. It was against that development which threatened the people's survival and led to natural and environmental destruction. The movement was also against profit making and consumerism and believed that the ultimate aim of the society should be human welfare and prosperity.

3.10 G.M.A.: An Assessment

In late 1990s G.M.A. got a setback when many front runner leaders joined mainstream politics. Besides this, the movement started picking up all the local and national issues that were not relevant for the movement. Because of lack of committed leadership, proper organisational setup and clear cut strategies and vision, G.M.A. lost somewhere and forgot its main aim.

But 1998-99 proved to be a very fruitful year for the movement because Bihar government abolished taxes from the Ganges region and announced that fisherfolk were the original owners of the water. But the conflict exists still in some districts of northern Bihar over the control of thousands of ponds, tanks, riverines, and drains. The traditional fisherfolk and other dalit castes, who live near the ponds, tanks and other water-logged areas, have begun to assert their fishing rights over them. The response from the members of forward castes, landlords and money lenders, who had controlled the wetlands for long, was violent. [26] In 1999, the district administration had made it clear that fishing rights in government-controlled ponds would be allotted through a leasing system. But the most common practice was to get the lease in the name of a fisherfolk or a dalit (Mushhar) who was heavily indebted to the landowner or the money lender. So the landowner/moneylender continues to control every activity including the sale of the catch. The same situation is still prevailing. However, the fishing community is trying hard to change the existing situation.

The Ganga Mukti Andolan has been so successful that the panidari system does not exist any more in its original form. But other exploitative systems related with fisheries are very much prevalent in different parts of Bihar. The fisherfolk and other dalit castes whose livelihood is from fishing, are waiting for the day when their traditional ownership on fishing will come back to them.

3.11Conclusion

The Ganga Mukti Andolan is an example of a successful environment movement in India. It is successful because panidari system does not exist any more in its original form. But other exploitative systems related with fisheries are prevalent in different parts of Bihar. Although G.M.A was finally a successful movement, it had seen many ups and downs and diversions because of lack of a clear cut vision and far sighted leaderhip. Since it was a local movement based on local problems/issues, the leadership was also very local and unorganized. The outsiders particularly the activists of Sampoona Kranti Andolan (Jay Prakash Narayan's) kept on joining the movement and leaving it also to join mainstream party politics. This movement never had an experienced and seasoned leader who could give it a proper and clear direction and organizational vision. This movement never gave importance to organisational set up, only the people who were affected and some sympathisers kept the movement alive. Sometimes the male members of the movement used to fight among themselves under the influence of alcohol on very petty issues and that weaken the strength of the movement.

The G.M.A started with the basic issue of survival of the fisherfolk but in due course it incorporated many other important environmental issues which were part of the national environmental discourse at that time. Those broad issues were the reasons for its diversions from the main issue.

This movement has a great social and environmental relevance and importance because it was fought on a very basic social issue. Every human being has an equal right for access to natural resources like air water. The G.M.A fought for it and got the right to use the Ganges water. This if is very important for a country like ours where a great number of people are deprived of so many basic human rights. This movement shows the way to other deprived people to fight for their rights. This movement is very significant from the environmental point of view also because in the process of long struggle, it took up many environmental related issues which made the poor illiterate, fisherfolk villagers aware about ecology, environment and related concerns. .This is an important contribution of the movement to environmental awareness.

Notes

1. One who used to collect land revenue.
2. Jalkar Zamindari is Hindi translation of Panidari.
3. Sri Bhairab Nath, Basudev and Shivajee are names of the God.
4. Yogendra and Safdar Imam Kadari, *Ganga Ko Abiral Bahane Do*, Ganga Mukti Andolan Publication, Bhagalpur, 1990, p-11.
5. A section of people having control over banks of the Ganges.
6. Ibid, p-12.
7. Ibid. p-12.
8. K. S. Belgrami, *Ganga ko Abiral Bahane Do*, Ganga Mukti Andolan Publication, Bhagalpur, 1990, p-88.
9. K. S. Bilgrami and J. S. Dutta Munshi, *Ecology of River Ganga: Patna to Farakka,* quoted from Ganga Ko Abiral Bahane Do, p-25.
10. Scale for measuring Hydrogen concentration of Ion.
11. Parts per million.

12. Aneeta Sharma, Ganga fish a health hazard, *The Times of India*, 12th March 2001.

13. Yogendra and Safdar Imam Kadari, *Ganga Ko Abiral Bahane Do*, Ganga Mukti Andolan Publication, Bhagalpur, 1990, p-19

14. Ibid, p-20

15. Ibid, p-20

16. Ibid, p-31

17. Ibid, p-31

18. Ibid, p-32

19. Ibid, p-32

20. Ibid, p-32

21. Ibid, p-32

22. Bio – Oxygen Demand is an index to measure the pollution level in the water.

23. Saibal Dasgupta, 'Pollution Persists in the Ganga near Varanasi', *The Times of India*, New Delhi, September 19, 1992.

24. As quoted in an *Australian Community Aid Abroad Aware Programme*, October 1989.

25. Ibid, p-59

26. Mukul Sharma, A Struggle for fishing rights, *Frontline*, July 16, 1999.

4

Suberna Rekha Andolan

After the second world war the industrialised world of west were trapped in deep economic crisis. They used poor Afro-Asian countries as market to sell their techniques and machines. Big dams were constructed in many countries to actualise these techniques. The Damodar and Koshi rivers were the first in South Bihar (now Jharkhand) where big dams were sanctioned in 1945. The practice of big dams got a fillip when the architect of modern India, Jawahar Lal Nehru who termed these dams as 'temples of modern India'.

In independent India, industrialisation was on the top of government's priority list. Making of big dams were also considered as a part of industrialisation. Gradually, people started feeling that big dams are not the right thing for Indian conditions. In the decade of 1970s some protests started against the big dams. People protested against big dams because it displaces the poor, women and the tribals. The Narmada Bachhao Andolan, Koel-Karo Andolan and Subernarekha Andolan are part of these protest movements.

Subernarekha means streak of gold. The Subernarekha river is an inter-state river flowing through the states of Jaharkhand, West Bengal and Orissa into the Bay of Bengal. Its catchment area is 18,950 square kilometers. About 70 percent of the catchment area is located in Bihar and it traverses a total distance of 395 kilometers (224 kilometers in Bihar, 64 kilometers in West Bengal, 62 kilometers in Orissa, 34 kilometers along Jharkhand-West Bengal border, 11 kilometers along Jharkhand-Orissa border). The river has its origin near Ranchi; while skirting Ranchi town it is still a rivulet. Gradually it acquires the dimensions of a full-fledged river. The river basin is bound on the north by Ranchi district (Jharkhand) and Purulia (West Bengal), on the east by Midnapur district (West Bengal), on the south by Kenjhore and Mayurbhanj district (Orissa) and on the west by Ranchi district (Jharkhand) and Sundergarh district (Orissa).

The population of India in 1981 was about 700 million, growing at an annual rate of 22 per cent per year. Agriculture was and remains the dominant sector in the Indian economy, employing about 70percent of the work force, providing about 45percent of India's exports and contributing about 40percent to gross national product. It had been government of India policy since independence to expand agriculture production in order to reduce India's dependence on imports and to raise the living standards of the rural poor. As a means of increasing production, the Government of India and the Indian states strove to expand the area under irrigation. Although irrigation development had proceeded rapidly, it became increasingly apparent that most schemes were performing much below their potential. This was due mainly to poor planning and designing of facilities, inadequate operation, unreliable water delivery and inequitable distribution to the farmers. Little irrigation had reached the most backward, hilly areas in the southern part of Bihar where the tribal population was concentrated.

It is in this background that the Subernarekha Multipurpose Project was evolved. The Subernarekha Multipurpose Project (SMP) formulated by Bihar Government aims at integrated development of the Subernarekha basin by harnessing the water resources of river Subernarekha for irrigation, flood control and municipal and industrial use. It is an inter-state project providing substantial flood control and irrigation benefits to Orissa, and similar benefits, though on a smaller scale, to West Bengal.

The development proposals for Subernarekha were submitted by Government of Bihar to Government of India as early as 1973. However, finalisation of these proposals and clearance for their implementation had to wait for an agreement among the three riparian states of then Bihar, Orissa and West Bengal on the sharing of Subernarekha waters and the manner of utilisation. Negotiations among the states were carried out in three bi-party agreements: first between the Chief Ministers of then Bihar and Orissa on 17th January 1976 at Patna; a second agreement on 25th October 1976 at Bhubaneshwar between the Chief Ministers of then Bihar and West Bengal and finally a Tripartite agreement concluded by the three Chief Ministers of then Bihar, Orissa and West Bengal on 7th August 1978 at New Delhi. "According to this agreement, the annual yield of the Subernarekha river at 75 percent dependability at Kokpara would be shared by then Bihar, Orissa and West Bengal in the proportion of 32:12:1 respectively. In case of surplus water over 75 percent dependable at Galudih, it will be shared in the ratio of 8:1:1 by then Bihar, Orissa and West Bengal respectively, while in case of shortage this ratio would be 32:1:1 respectively." [1]

The SMP was included in the Tribal sub-plan of then Bihar. The project had undergone some changes by way of (a) addition in the scope of irrigation from Chandil dam by a right bank canal and (b) inclusion of a number of small hydel schemes. The estimated cost of the project as cleared by Central Water Commission at 1981 price level was Rs. 4,809 million which had been revised by the project authorities to Rs. 12,700 million in 1989. The newly conceived Chandil Right Bank Canal System was estimated to cost Rs.605 million and the hydro-electric schemes Rs. 650 million. Taking these new schemes into account, the integrated cost of modified SMP came to Rs. 13,955 million. The SMP was posed for soft loan assistance to World Bank leading to an IDA Credit Agreement for a four year time slice between 1982-83 to 1985-86 which stipulated World Bank financing to the tune of 127 million US dollars. The World Bank subsequently agreed to extend the period of reimbursement from June 1986 to June 1988, and finally the closing date of the first time Slice Credit Agreement was extended to April 1989.

The main objectives of Subernarekha Multipurpose Project were – (i) to provide a reliable water supply for irrigation to about 1,60,000, 90,000 and 5,000 hectares (total 2,55,000 hectare) of Cultivable Command Area in then Bihar, Orissa and West Bengal respectively; (ii) to provide water for municipal and industrial use mainly in then Bihar (particularly to Jamshedpur steel city) and (iii) to reduce flood damages in Orissa and West Bengal. When World Bank's Supervisory Committee came for supervision at the river site, it recommended a 'hydro electric power project' at Chandil dam. So, Subernarekha Multipurpose Project got an additional objective of producing electricity also.

The SMP comprised essentially of four units viz – (i) Chandil dam [2], (ii) Icha dam, (iii) Kharkai barrage [3] and (iv) Galudih barrage. All these four units were independent in themselves and were capable of providing partial benefits to their respective command areas.

It was estimated that on completion, the project will generate employment equivalent to about 1,63,000 full time jobs in an area where employment to agriculture labour is not available for nine months in a year. The construction of the project till completion will generate avenues for labour employment of 8 to 9 million mandays per year till 1993.

4.1 Demography and Local Details

It is important here to know the demography and other local details before the reasons for the birth of the movement and other issues. In the Chandil reservoir area the tribal population is approximately 24.5percent of the total tribal population. In Subernarekha region majority of the population are Santhals followed by HOS, Bhumijs and Mundas. Of the remaining population, a small percentage belong to the scheduled castes and high caste Hindus. Owing to the proximity of the reservoir area to Bengal, most of the people understand and speak Bengali. They also speak a language known as Kurmali which is quite akin to Bengali.

The bulk of the agricultural land is held by the higher castes followed by the backwards. Most of the scheduled castes have either tiny holdings or landless. Economically, they are tied to the large land holders. The relationship which has grown over the centuries is perceptible even at present times. Despite urbanisation and growth of industry in and around the steel city of Jamshedpur, over 75 per cent of the people still depend on agriculture and allied activities for their livelihood. The present occupational pattern of the workers in the submergence area are like this: the cultivators 50.37 per cent, agricultural labourers 25.26 per cent, those involved in household industry 3.00 per cent and those engaged in miscellaneous occupations 21.37 percent.

The average literacy percentage in this area as per 1981 census is 27 per cent for male and about 5.7 per cent for female. The institutions which will go under submergence are mainly temples, asthanas and sarnas. Sarna is a place with cluster of trees which is used as a place of worship by tribals. Asthanas are the places where lower caste people worship. The educational institutions like 3 high schools, 4 middle schools and 11 primary schools would also come under submergence area when the dam get ready.

When SMP project was launched, it was widely publicised that it was basically an irrigation project. The productivity of this region will grow further. It was claimed that after completion of the project the yield of rice would increase more than thrice. Around 2.10 lakh tons of wheat can be produced that is not produced even today. In addition to this, crops like potato, soyabean, sugercane etc. can be produced. It was also claimed that after completion of the project only 23percent family would remain below poverty line.

According to the government report the primary objective of the SMP is irrigation. It is true that the total irrigated area in this district is very negligible, about 3.5 per cent of the total cultivated area. Today irrigation is the sole excuse for the existence of so many departments and projects in the tribal areas of then Bihar like the Irrigation Department, Minor Irrigation Department, Water Ways Department and many others. According to a reliable source, more than 50 crores of rupees have gone down the drain during the last several years in the name of irrigation projects in Singhbhum.

SMP intends to irrigate the tribal lands through a network of canals. Past experience has shown that canal irrigation is most unsuitable for this area which is very sloping and undulating. Under the pretext of this project, vast areas of good agricultural lands belonging to the tribals were acquired by the project officials from both sides of the canal. The surplus land was then leased out to the friends of the officials for some years. Now they are being used for building colonies for non-tribal officers and employees. For most of the months in a year, there is no water at all in the canal.

Supply of industrial and municipal water to the many growing industrial centres in this mineral and timber rich tribal district is the real purpose of SMP. After the construction of SMP the whole of Singhbhum district would have witnessed a very rapid and gigantic industrialization and modernization process for the exploitation of its natural and human resources. This process had already started with the beginning of the construction of a huge sponge iron plant by the Modi Group at Chandil. In short, there would have been an industrial explosion in Singhbhum. There was a fear among the local people that there would be an unprecedented assault on the relatively stable and self-sufficient indigenous people and their land and other resources. It will not only mean a further dispossession of their sustainable resources but it would also lead to their brutal displacement, pollution and degradation of their environment.

The SMP will also bring about a type of 'green revolution' in the command area of the project. As one writer wrote in a daily, "The Subernarekha project is going to transform its command area into a virtual 'gold yielding' region". [4] But the local people were not in agreement of this view. SMP was already causing a tremendous influx of outsiders to Singhbhum. The various benefits arising out of the project were being taken away mostly by these outsiders. The indigenous and displaced people were getting only unskilled and exploitative jobs. After completion SMP will be controlled by the dominant industrial interests rather than by the farmers, it is the needs of the largely urban-industrial consumers rather than those of the indigenous rural agriculturalists that will take precedence. The interests of indigenous people, in effect, are being ignored on the altar of India's industrialization and modernization.

Though the project report of the irrigation department, Government of then Bihar paints a rosy picture regarding SMP, it fails to impress the indigenous people of Singhbhum, the people who are most affected by the project. They considered the project as a curse rather than a blessing and protested against it in many different ways. The reasons for their resistance can be summarised in this way.

4.2 Dispossession of the Indigenous People

The situation facing the indigenous people of Singhbhum due to the construction of SMP is the same as the situation of other parts of Indian people who are faced with similar development projects. The basic problem that characterizes their situation is dispossession. They are systematically and methodically being dispossessed of the ownership of their means of production, of the product of their labour and of the very means of human existence. In the name of national interest and 'progress' they are being dispossessed of their culture, their values, their very identity and their community. The indigenous people are being dispossessed economically, socially, politically and culturally.

The price that the indigenous people of Singhbhum will have to pay for the project in terms of their ancestral land, to which their entire life is very closely linked, is enormous. For the construction of the two dams, two barrages, seven canals having a total length of 342 kilometers, 712 kilometers of roads, and for the many colonies for housing the officers and other employees of the project, vast areas of land belonging to the indigenous people are being acquired by the government. According to the project report on land acquisition and survey (April 1985), for the Chandil dam alone a total of 43,500 acres of land will have to be acquired. Large areas of *Gairmazarua* lands all over Singhbhum are being taken over by the government and colonies are being constructed there to house the project personnels. These *Gairmazarua* lands are the common property of the local people on which they graze their cattle. Due to the building of these colonies the indigenous people are deprived of these common property resources. Further, about 10,000 acres of forests on which the local people depend for their livelihood, will be wiped out because of the project.

The Chhotanagpur Tenancy Act (CNT) prohibits the alienation of tribal land to non-tribals. In spite of the restrictions given in the CNT Act large areas of tribal lands are being legally and illegally alienated by the vested interests. The state and its administration instead of protecting the poor tribals have become a major party to these alienations. The SMP also has given a golden opportunity for the vested interests to alienate large areas of tribal land in Singhbhum. In the name of flood control a vast area of tribal land is being acquired for the Chandil dam. This dam is supposed to have a provision for 10 feet of water for flood cushion. This might submerge a large tract of land just for a few hours or for a maximum period of 24 to 48 hours during the year. [5] For this purpose the authorities are acquiring vast areas of extra land (more than 37,500 acres) belonging to the tribals.

4.3 Displacement of the People

The Chandil reservoir will submerge 32 villages fully and 84 villages partially in Chandil, Nimdih and Ichagarh blocks displacing a total of 6,773 families. "Out of this lower castes families will be 444 Adivasi families will be 1,791 Scheduled castes / tribes will be 4,164 and others will be 374 households. The total number of people that would have been displaced is 37,600". [6] The Survey work in some areas are not done otherwise the number of families to be displaced would be much higher.

Due to the construction of Icha Dam on the Kharkai river in the Kolhan area 21,000 acres of settlement will be wiped out. In effect 20 villages will completely disappear from the map and 41 villages partially in Chaibasa, Tantnagar and Rajnagar blocks displacing 5,600 families. Most of the families affected by the Icha dam belong to HO tribe. The HOs form the majority in

Kolhan. [7] In fact Kolhan is also known as HO disum or the land of the HOs.

The affected people are not happy with the policy of compensation adopted by the government. The displaced people are being paid for their land and house only. And the compensation is given in monetary terms. [8] In the beginning the rate of compensation fixed by the government was very low. Sometimes, as low as Rs.200 per acre had been paid on the basis of sale deed patta. After a long struggle and protest by the people the rate was raised and it varied from Rs.5000 to Rs.30,000 per acre depending on the type of land. The classification of land was done on the basis of yield and land tax tokens were taken as indicators of quality of land. Since compensation was paid on the basis of tax tokens, they got a smaller amount than they should be getting for their land. The actual compensation paid was much less than the promised rate. As for example, at villages Chaliama, Bankasai and Tolai altogether 22.63 acres of land were acquired after paying a compensation of Rs.88,406. This worked out to be Rs.3,484 per acre. Again in village Kesargadia 406 acres were acquired from 303 land owners after paying a sum of Rs.5,71,771 which works out to be Rs.1,408 per acre. [9]

For the indigenous people monetary compensation had very little value. First of all, it was very meagre and inadequate for their rehabilitation as they were not able to buy land in other places at the prevailing high rates. The price of land had also gone up because of the demand for land by displaced people. Secondly, since the only skill they had was farming, they were not able to put the money for any commercial use. Since most of them were illiterates, they were cheated even by the officials, who made the payments. Many reports of bribes had been reported in the press. Having resided in and around forests and vacant lands for centuries, many had no proof of legal ownership. According to a report which appeared in *Amrit Bazar Patrika* of 9th March 1986, more than 100 adivasi families belonging to the Savar and Kharia tribes in village Bedia who had been living there for more than half a century were served with a government notice to vacate the place or to face penalty under Bihar Public Land Eviction Act, 1956.

Cash compensation had also created mistrust and division in many families which were otherwise living peacefully. Some 'cleverer' and 'stronger' members of the families had fraudulently deprived the weaker ones like widows and old women of their proper compensation and misappropriated it for themselves. This was done in connivance with the officials who took bribes for such illegal acts. As far as the indigenous people were concerned, cash compensation was not only inadequate but practically useless in the long run. They needed cultivable land for their survival. This had also been recommended by the Tribal Welfare Commissioner, Ranchi in a confidential report sent to the government of Bihar regarding SMP and the atrocities committed on adivasis. [10]

In a study, Paul Fernandes of the Xavier Labour Relations Institute, Jamshedpur on the rehabilitation programme of SMP, suggested that for effective rehabilitation one acre of agricultural land with irrigation facilities should be provided so that at least two crops could be cultivated, or two acres of cultivable land should be provided so that at least one crop during monsoon could be cultivated. [11] The state government had formulated a 10-point programme of rehabilitation that seemed highly unsatisfactory. The future of 12,000 and more families comprised more than 75,000 indigenous people were displaced by SMP was really very bleak. In fact, most of them do not know where they will go. The reports about the miserable condition of displaced have been appearing in the newspapers.

The government's rehabilitation policy did not take proper care of cultural values, traditions and the very survival needs of the people to be displaced. It has resulted in the destruction of their identity and in their ultimate pauperization.

Providing employment to the displaced families was the most untrue promise of the whole rehabilitation programme. The government had promised that priority would be given to the displaced people in the appointment of fourth grade employees and at least 50 per cent of the third grade positions would also be given to them. The study conducted by Paul Fernandes showed that the percentage of displaced people employed in the project as fourth grade employees was less than ten percent of the jobs available and in the third grade the percentage employed was less than five percent. The number of displaced people actually employed in jobs like earth cutting, loading, carrying were also not many. The contractors preferred to employ workers from outside so that they can exploit them maximum. Even child labourers were employed by these contractors. They were brought from Orissa. Many reports had come up in the press regarding the exploitation of workers in SMP and non-employment of displaced and local people. The *Press Trust of India* also reported that over 30 percent families displaced by the execution of SMP had been neither rehabilitated nor were provided any compensation. [12] However, government policy promised that all educated unemployed would be absorbed in the project or would be given alternative employment but outsiders were being employed in the project ignoring the interests of the local people.

The dispossession of the indigenous people of Singhbhum due to SMP was taking place not only in the economic sphere but it was also affecting social and cultural spheres. Their family life was getting disrupted. They were losing their traditional social controls, and social tension was increasing among them. They were becoming more vulnerable to diseases and emotional disorders. Many social evils like alcoholism, crime, suicide, prostitution, delinquency and despair had suddenly gone up. They confronted with development and modernization, experiencing a loss of self-esteem. Every area of their life from marriage to language, customs and religion had come under attack. Language is the main factor that expresses the identity of a community. With the coming of the outsiders, because of the project, their language was highly polluted now.

4.4 Protest Movement against SMP

The local people started protesting against this project right from its beginning. In the beginning it was an unorganised movement but since 1978 it became an effective movement. The Forward Block was heading it at that time. The Forward Block took out a big procession against this project on 26th March 1978 from Chandil to Chandlengi. The local member of Legislative Assembly Ghanshyam Mahato was leader of this movement. After the procession it was decided that the activists will sit for fast undo death from 23rd April 1978. It was well participated by the local people. On 29th April, 1978 deputy Commissioner of Singhbhum visited the site with heavy police force and ordered to demolish the dharna camp. The people were arrested and beaten up badly. A Gandhian freedom fighter Bimlendu Das Gupta who was eighty years old was badly injured.

Again on 30th April thousands of people gathered at the same place ; a majority of them were women. Without any formal talk, the Magistrate ordered his men to open tear gas and later to fire at the crowd. About twenty people died on the spot. After that for sometime the movement was scattered and could not make its presence felt.

The leadership of this movement went into the hands of a retired military man of Eligarha village under Singhbhum district. Ganga Ram Kalundiya came to his village after retirement when he came to know about the project. He started mobilising the people and uniting them against the SMP.

This mobilisation turned into processions and demonstrations. On 3rd April 1982 thousands of people demonstrated against Subernarekha Multipurpose Project in front of the project office at Chaliyama. Procession was peaceful but in an attacking mood. The moment processionists reached the project office the police started chasing them away. Some of them were badly beaten up by the police. The people scuffled with the police. Ganga Ram Kalundiya was not present in the procession, but the police was desperately looking for him. The people who were present in the demonstration sensed something wrong and suggested Ganga Ram Kalundiya to be careful and attentive in the night. Since he had not done anything wrong so he took these suggestions casually. But villagers planned to be watchful in the night and if any thing went wrong, they decided that would beat the drums. The noise of the drums would work as an alarm. At 4'0' clock in the morning when villagers thought the police will not come, suddenly police marched to the Eligarha village and surrounded Ganga Ram's house. The police entered his house, injured his legs and arrested him. The villagers beat the drums and people gathered at his house. The people were ready to attack the police with bows and arrows. They formed a circle to stop the police for arresting Ganga Ram Kalundiya. But he was arrested. The police attacked villagers also. They got dispersed in different directions and in the meantime police fired at Ganga Ram from the back. Police was able to establish that they had to fire because he was running away from the police custody. He was taken to Singhbhum. The villagers also followed him but they could not find out his whereabouts. Next day a Sub Divisional Magistrate came to Eligarha village and told the villagers to collect Ganga Ram's corpse from Singhbhum.

It was a shocking and horrifying incident for the tribals of the whole Kolhan region. He was killed by the police personnel of the same government which has rewarded him 'Bravery Award' for his role in India-China war. For three-four months the whole area was terrorised but gradually the people again stood up to protest against SMP in a more organised way. On 21st October 1982 hundreds of youth organised and took out a procession in front of Block Development Officer of Echagarh under the banner of Krantikari Kshetriya Yuva Morcha. In the police fire Ajit Mahto and Dhananjay Mahto were killed on the spot, three persons were seriously injured and forty people were arrested and sent to jail. The government's policy of suppressing the movement proved a boon in disguise for the activists of the movement. The more the government was trying to suppress them, the more they got united with greater strength. They started celebrating 4th April as Martyr Day every year. They organised big public rallies and repeated their oath that the dam should not be constructed at any cost. The protests against the dam were continuing at different places of the region. At this time Brahma Deo Sharma of Jan Vikas Andolan,

Ghanshyam of Jay Prakash Andolan and many different organisations got involved in this movement.

In February 1991 a big conference against the disaster brought about by big dams and the concept of development was organised for the first time. It was organised in Kuju (dam site) where Bihar Mukti Andolan, Chhatra-Yuva Sangharsh Vahini, Mahila Sangharsh Vahini, Munda Manaki Sangh, Icha Kharkai Visthapith Sangh, Sampoorna Kranti Manch, Santhal Pargana Bachao Manch and many other organisations, groups and individuals participated. As per the decision of the conference, *Satyagraha* (firmness in adhering to truth) against the construction of the dam started from 5th April 1991. The Chief Administrator with the then Commissioner of Singhbhum visited the Dharna site at 9'o' clock in the night; and arrested more than hundred activists and sent them to jail. Half of the arrested activists were women. This news spread like fire in villages and hundreds of people started coming for arrest. It included men, women, youth and old. The arrest continued till 15th April and all the jails in then Southern Bihar became overcrowded.

On 28th April 1991 in Jagannathpur village of Chaibasa district a conference was organised with the slogan of 'Apna Gaon Apna Raj' (our village, our administration) in protest against the dam. Brahma Deo Sharma and other activists of national level participated in this conference. On 13th May a big procession was organised for the release of the jailed activists and in protest against the dam. The procession culminated in a public meeting where activists, leaders, journalists and theatre personalities of different parts of the country participated. In the first week of July, Chhatra Yuva Sangharsh Vahini under the leadership of Balram organised a fast on the issue of displacement at Chandil.

When Balram's situation got deteriorated, administration agreed to accept their demands. On 8th August 1991 Jharkhand Mukti Andolan, Mahila Sangharsh Vahini, Chhatra-Yuva Sangharsh vahini, Echa Kharkai Visthapith Sangh and other friendly organisations staged a dharna for eight hours to protest against the project in front of Chaibasa deputy Commissioner. On the 10th death anniversary of Ganga Ram Kalundiya i.e. 4th April 1992 it was decided to intensify the agitation. In addition to different organisations which were supporting the movement, some other organisations like Kolhan Raksha Sangh and All Bihar Students Union also joined in this cause. A *padayatra* from Eligarha (then Bihar) to Baripada (Orissa) was organised to make the people of the affected area aware and get involved in this movement. It was organised from 5th April to 13th April 1992. To make the movement more broad and discuss the experiences of different other movements, a two days conference on 'Jamin Bachhao' was organised in Jamshedpur.

During the eight days *padayatra*, they addressed the villagers of every village they crossed. There used to be a cultural programme during their night stay. The theme of all the songs and plays performed there were against the dam and in favour of *Jal, Jungle* and *Zameen* (water, forest and land). The leaders of the padayatra raised many broader issues in their addresses. They not only objected to the construction of big dams but also expressed reservations about the very concept of development. According to them all these developmental schemes meant for tribals, farmers and poor always proved disastrous for them. They believe that displaced people forget their culture, civilization, traditional economic system and community life.

On 7th and 8th November 1992 they organised a conference in Jamshedpur. It was attended by writers, activists, journalists, jurists and environmentalists. The theme of the conference was Zameen Bachao (save the land). Again on 4th April in 1993 'Shaheed Ganga Ram Kalundiya Mela' was organised in Eligarha. By this time the movement took a very serious turn and it seemed that the construction of the dam was not possible. Because of international pressure, World Bank announced its withdrawal in sponsoring Subernarekha Multipurpose Project. The activists of the movement celebrated it as their great victory. On 11th June 1993 a victory procession was brought out in Chaibasa that culminated in a public meeting. It was emphasised in the meeting that it was just the beginning and not the end of the fight.

They reiterated their oath to not allowing the dam to be completed. Every year on 4th April they organise public meetings, processions and many other activities to commemorate Ganga Ram's sacrifice and to mobilise themselves. Gradually they started widening their issues. They started asking for Apna Gaon Mein Apna Raj (Our own Rule in our village) in the entire Kolhan-Bihar region, that the demand for Manaki-Munda System and Wilkinson's Rules [13] should be reimplemented in this region. Manaki-Munda System is a local form of administration. Mundas are the heads of the villages while Manakies are the heads of the Mundas. Mundas are elected by the villagers and Manakies are elected by the Mundas. But once they are elected generally their sons take over after their father's death. They look after the whole affairs of the village. This Munda-Manaki system had been accepted by the post independence legal system.

T. Wilkinson was an agent of the first Governor General of South Western Frontier in 1834. He studied the social norms and traditions of tribal belt and formulated thirty one rules for the tribals and passed it to the central government for acceptance. It was passed by the government in 1938 and was applicable even after independence. But in 1969 Bihar government by its regulation-I scrapped the Wilkinson's rule and deprived the tribals of their rights. They went to the court. The Ranchi Bench of Patna High court vide C.W.J.C. No. 338 of 1985 (R) accepted and recognised this Manki Munda System. The judgement says Bihar government's executive powers would not be applicable in Kolhan region where Wilkinson's rules were followed.

The tribals of this region kept on fighting for the tribals self rule under the leadership of Brahma Deo Sharma (B. D. Sharma). A Committee was set up under the chairpersonship of Dilip Singh Bhuria. The Bhuria Committee submitted its report to the parliament. On 24th December 1996 it became a law. According to this law, tribal's traditions would be acknowledged and all power would lay with the Gram Sabha. It authorised Mundas and Manakies System to continue.

The movement got a slump at this point because the SMP was withdrawn by the government. Also other demands of the indigenous people like Mundas and Manakies system were realised. So people got diverted into different types of struggles under the leadership of various political and other groups like the Jharkhand Mukti Morcha, Kolhan Raksha Sangh, Jharkhand Mukti Andolan, Icha Kharkai Visthapit Sangh. The demand for a separate Jharkhand state became the major demand of this region and all activists of SMP joined the movement for the Jharkhand State. It took many years, many ups and downs, many political permutations and combinations. Different political parties took different stands, sometimes completely changing from their earlier stands, keeping in mind the vote bank and elections. Finally the central government formed a separate Jharkhand state in the year 2000. The activists of SMP are now fighting for different social issues; some of them have joined the mainstream parliamentary politics.

4.5 Conclusion

The Suberna Rekha Andolan in another successful environmental movement in contemporary India. It is successful because construction of S.M.P. was stopped after its protest. From the very beginning, its leadership had a very clear vision about the goal. All those people who were the leaders of the movement at different points of time were very sincere and committed. They had been able to organize the affected people in a better way. Subernrekha Andolan never got diverted from its main issue and never took up any other issue till World Bank withdrew the construction of SMP.

The Subernrekha Andolan also proves the hypothesis of this study that all Indian environmental movements are based on/centred around the issue of the very survival of the people.

Another significant aspect of the movement was the involvement of national level social activities and the sponsorship from the World Bank. The existing situation of the country at that time always kept the movement in the national and international news. This movement was well organized and focused. The prevention of the construction of the dam was the central concern of all the cultural programmes like songs, dances and plays.

The achievement of Subernrekha Andolan is very significant from the social and environmental point. It is significant because it fought for the very basic human rights of the tribals and poor – the right to live where they want. Due to the long duration of struggle, the activists of this movement learnt how to fight with the state machinery and how to keep the movement alive. That is perhaps how the activists of this movement were able to get the new state Jharkhand.

Notes

1. Environmental Impact Assessment and Planning for Environmental Management in Subernrekha Multipurpose Project, Bihar. A report by Metaplanners and Management Consultants, Patna, June 1990.
2. Dam is storage of water.
3. Barrage is Diversion of water.
4. I.M, Jha, *The Indian Nation*, 4th September, 1987, Patna.
5. Ibid.
6. Mathew Areeparampil, The impact of Subernarekha Multipurpose Project on the Indigenous People of *Singhbhum, People and Dams*, Society for Participatory Research in Asia, New Delhi.
7. Term used for tribal belt by the British Government.
8. Anjum Arvind – *Subernrekha Ka Aahvan* Visthapit, Mukti Vahini, A 4/85, A Road, Telco Colony, Jamshedpur, p-4
9. Raj, Aloysius, "Kharkai Bandh Ban Jane Se Kolhan Ka Astitva Hi Mit Jayega", *Singhbhum Ekta*, Vol. VIII, No. 10, 21st December 1985.
10. Sunila Basant, confidential report No.1247 sent to the Commissioner and Secretary, Home Department, Old Secretariat, Bihar, Patna, 5th June 1982.
11. Paul Fernandes, *Subernarekha Multipurpose Project: Towards Evolving a strategy for the management of Displaced families*, XLRI, Jamshedpur, 1985.

12. Mathew Areeparampil, The Impact of Subernarekha Multipurpose Project On the Indigenous People of Singhbhum, *People and Dams*, Society for Participatory Research in Asia, New Delhi.

13. Rules for the administration of Civil Justice within the jurisdiction of the Agent to the Governor-General under Regulation XIII of 1833.

5

Alternate Development and Social Action

Bertrand Russell and Albert Einstein issued a 'manifesto' in 1955 that "There lies before us, if we choose, continual progress in happiness, knowledge and wisdom." The appeal, addressed mainly to the scientists of the world, ended thus:

We appeal as human beings to human beings: remember your humanity, and forget the rest. If you can do so, the way lies open to a new paradise, if you cannot there lies before us the risk of universal death.

But the promise of continual progress and the way to a new paradise does not seem to be so clear. Rather it seems more vague and remote. There is a need to rethink the very premises on which the modern industrial civilization has been based. This is a matter of great concern why human progress has been held up or distorted and diverted into wrong channels. The basic reason lies in modern man's approach to science and technology. The prevailing technology that is producing more and more deadly armaments is also producing a more wasteful civilization. The modern science and technology have flourished and has given rise to a world structure that has become increasingly iniquitous and conflict-ridden, and in the process millions of human beings are becoming deprived, dislocated and their life redundant.

The places where modern science and technology have introduced themselves in wasteful ways of human consumption are not limited to the rich, highly industrialised, 'developed' North; they are also to be found in the poorer, less industrialized, 'underdeveloped' South.

The social system based on capitalist mode of production is found to be unsatisfactory. The socialist system also is recognised as unsatisfactory. The third world thus emerged as a coherent human experience which neither approved capitalism nor state socialism. An alternative is currently being evolved through intense deliberation and debate – as a common alternative to both the first and the second worlds.

The very concept of alternatives is not to be limited just to development policies. It should entail visions about society and polity; it should do this in the context of the evolution of the human community as a whole. Alternative is a conception not just in the theory of development. It entails a model of world order and the transformations entailed for such a world order. It is an exercise in values and their realisation at various levels of reality.

Indian environmental movements are fighting for an alternative model that should not challenge the very survival of rural poor, tribals and women. Their basic objection is against the development model that India adopted after independence and created 'two' nations within one nation.

5.1 Complexity in Development Model

After a long struggle, India became independent in 1947. Development of the nation and improvement of the lives of its citizens were the immediate goals of our leaders. From its inception, the Indian state was confronted by two different visions of development: The Gandhian notion of reviving the village economy and the Nehruvian model of rapid industrialization. Gandhi wrote a letter to Nehru on 5th October 1945, in which he described his dream of free India:

"I believe that, if India is to attain true freedom, and through India the world as well, then sooner or later we will have to live in villages – in huts, not in palaces. A few billion people can never live happily and peaceably in cities and palaces. My villages exist today in my imagination. The villager in this imagined village will not be apathetic. He will not lead his life like an animal in a squalid dark room. Men and women will live freely and be prepared to face the whole world. The village will not know cholera, plague or small pox. No one will live indolently, nor luxuriously. After all this, I can think of many things which will have to be produced on a large scale. May be there will be railways, so also post and telegraph. What it will have and what it will not, I do not know. Nor do I care. If I can maintain the essence, the rest will mean free facility to come and settle. And if I leave the essence, I leave everything." [1]

Gandhi's letter could not change the mind of Jawaharlal Nehru. He replied Gandhi's letter of October 1945:

"It is many years since I read *Hind Swaraj* and I have only a vague picture in my mind. But even when I read it twenty or more years ago it seemed to me completely unreal. A village, normally speaking, is backward intellectually and culturally and no progress can be made from a backward environment". [2]

In addition to Nehru most of the Indian leaders were of the view that India should adopt the western path of development which is based on science, technology and industrialization. It is in this ideological background India adopted the 'industrialize or perish' model of economic development in the Second Five Year Plan. "From the Second Plan onwards, the Indian government spent only 22 percent of its total plan budget on agriculture, even though 75 percent of the population was engaged in agriculture. The greater share of plan outlay consistently went to develop industries, which employed merely 11 per cent of the population". [3] When this policy was adopted it was assumed that the benefits of industrialization, increased production, employment and income would trickle down to the economy at the lowest level of the society. But this has not happened.

This model of development has changed two important bases of production: land and water. According to a study done by Centre for Science and Environment, 'in 1990, India had a land area of 328.7 million hectares, 55.6 percent of which was considered arable. 45.68 million hectares (ha) or 25 percent of arable land is irrigated'. [4] According to B.B. Vohra, "only 42 percent of the area demarcated as 'forest' is actually under adequate tree or grass cover; the rest is more or less completely devoid of vegetation". [5] According to the National Remote Sensing Agency, "forests covered 55.5 million ha (16.89 per cent of total land area) in 1972-75. During 1980-82, this area dropped to 46 million ha (14.1 per cent of total area). In the 1990s forests cover a scant 32.8 million ha or 10 percent of the total land area. Whereas four million hectares of forest area was lost between 1951 to 1976, over the last fifteen years 22.7 million hectares of forest have been cut down". [6]

Surprisingly these losses are not mentioned in our national income accounting. When we calculate our gross national product or our rate of industrial growth, costs like the loss of wasted land are not included in the calculus of economic decision-making. In fact, paradoxically environmental destruction is considered as a positive phenomenon if it provides a one-time increase in production, even though that increase may harm all possible future benefits and may have disastrous present side effects. For instance, deforestation will increase gross national product through the sale of timber, but there is no reimbursement of the losses incurred by cutting trees – the adverse ecological effects or the loss of other use values derived from a forest. The deforestation not only hampers the environment but also adversely affects economy of the poor and tribals. According to a UNDP report, "around 750 million of the world's poorest people live in rural areas. Of these, around 20 to 30 million move each year to town and cities. And an increasing proportion of these migrants are 'environmental refugees' whose land is so eroded or exhausted that it can no longer support them." [7] As ecological destruction disproportionately affects the poor, the state of India's Environment Report says that 'environmental degradation and social injustice are two sides of the same coin.'

Ironically most of the development policies, justified in the national interest, actually harm poor people's ability to control and use natural resources. The development model established since independence has fundamentally altered the way in which different social groups use and have access to natural resources. The changes wrought by the independent state have created conflicts over competing claims to the environment.

The objective of development should be to achieve minimum conditions of material welfare for all the people. The 'minimum' should be defined according to local conditions and norms. All of them should provide at least a package of minimum items of human necessity such as food, clothing, shelter and nutritional needs to children and mothers in particular. It should also provide socially approved health, education, drinking water and public transportation for all. An individual should not be only entitled to a minimum standard of living; he should also be able to participate actively in the way things are produced and decisions are made.

Our economic process which is sometimes also referred to as the industrial-bureaucratic nexus of modern society, should be prevented from destroying every other value in its inexporable march. In other words, as the values of a participatory democracy and of non-violence in man's relation to man and to the environment are joined with the values of individual autonomy and social justice. It is clear that the current model of modernisation is not conducive to nation's goals. The norm of a necessary shift from a predominantly rural to a predominantly urban structure based on large-scale industrialisation may not be the best thing that human intelligence has devised. It may turn into a structure of manipulation, exploitation and destruction of the very properties of natural environment that are essential to human survival.

5.2 Alternate Model of Development: Theoretical Issues

The concern with 'environment' and 'development' is significant only in this larger political context and in the context of the intellectual necessity of redefining the whole purpose of development. It will entail the search for an alternative model of development based not on specialised concerns of experts and aggregations there of, but on something that is at once more comprehensive and more accessible to all human beings. It must promote a view of human welfare.

The United Nations Conference on the Human Environment convened at Stockholm in June 1972 coined a new term "Ecodevelopment" to describe a process of ecologically sound development of positive management of the environment for human benefit. Almost after ten years, there was a growing recognition that 'many of the great problems of the world environment have political roots.'

In India, there is a major problem with entire range of activities and concerns: it does not appear to be based on a holistic understanding of the relationship between environment and development process. They seem to be based on the belief that concern for the environment essentially means protecting and conserving it, partly from development programmes but mainly from the people themselves. There is little effort to modify the development process itself in a manner that will bring it into greater harmony with the needs of the people and with the need to maintain ecological balance while increasing the productivity of our land, water and forest resources.

The post-independence political debate in India has centred on two major issues: equity and growth. The environmental concern has added a third dimension: sustainability. India's biggest challenge today is to identify and implement a development process that will lead to greater equity, growth and sustainability.

When we talk about alternative kind of development, it means a technology which is more welfare-oriented. In the Indian context the economist, Ernest Fritz Schumacher coined the expression "intermediate technology". [8] He wrote: "it requires no lengthy argument to agree that India is 'long' in labour and 'short' in capital. This means that she requires a level of technology, or 'capital investment per workplace', that is likely to be very different from that current in the western countries which are 'long' in capital and 'short' in labour.

Intermediate technology, according to Schumacher ought to fulfil four conditions. Firstly, the workplace should be created in areas in which people now live rather than being concentrated primarily in cities. Secondly they should be cheap enough to be created in large numbers without requiring large amounts of capital investment or of imports. The production techniques as well as the related methods of organisations involved must be relatively simple, with only a moderate degree of skill required for their successful operation, and finally production should be mainly from local materials and intended for local use.

The focus of alternative technology is not only a move away from the big, highly mechanised systems to smaller, decentralised ones; it is also a method of production which is in harmony with nature. Schumacher wrote, "Modern man does not experience himself as a part of nature but as an outside force destined to dominate and conquer it." [9] Marx himself had put it more eloquently: 'Nature is his body, with which he must remain in continuous intercourse if he is not to die'.

Amulya Reddy of ASTRA in Bangalore sums up well. About 'development' he says, 'Development is an ongoing process of social transformation, based on willing mass participation and control by the people over the decision-making process, using fully all the natural resources of a given society while maintaining the ecological balance of nature and in which the benefits of growth go first to the most needy, and, in which, over time, there is a reduction of all forms of inequality.'

India's biggest challenge today is to identify and implement a development process that will lead to greater equity, growth and sustainability. Large dams are in controversy in India today compelling the planners to think about an alternative in irrigation and power projects. In this context some alternatives have been suggested. The term alternative is used here to mean alternatives in the general thrust of the existing policies, which are at present tilted towards irrigation by large dams. All these alternatives are inspired by 'small is beautiful' and 'alternative technologies' schools of development. Apart from large dams and tubewells, other forms of irrigation that need to be considered for further development are small dams, tanks, water harvesting methods, traditional canal systems, ground water irrigation through wells.

5.3 Alternatives to Big Dams

It is being advocated by the 'alternate development' school that small dams have considerable advantage over large dams.

Small dams or check dams, with or without the provision of hydel power generation are considered by many a 'sustainable' alternative. A small / check dam can be constructed by putting a concrete block on the river stream to store water in a few acres of land. Generally this storage not only provides irrigation for kharif and rabi crops, but also helps in the recharging of groundwater. In addition to agricultural development, they play an important role in the regeneration of trees, bushes and grass. Small dams are cheaper also than large dams because it involves local labour and locally available material. Small dams are not as yet attached to the market forces and agricultural technology so they benefit the peasants. However, the large dam lobby always point out shortcomings and limitations of small dams. They argue that a large volume of water will be lost by evaporation in small reservoirs compared to large reservoirs where water depths are considerable. Large scale storage of water has its own problem of water loss due to waterlogging.

There are enough empirical evidences to substantiate that small dams are better options than large dams. According to a study conducted by Centre for Science and Environment, Vanvasi Sewa Ashram, a voluntary organisation in Mirzapur, has constructed around 750 small dams, each costing about Rs.60,000 and irrigating about 40 acres of land. This has completely changed the lifestyle of the local people and also regenerated vegetation in the region.

In spite of the encouraging results, small dams are neglected by the Indian state. It is because of limited scope of money making for engineers, contractors, politicians and bureaucrats. In a country like India big irrigation projects are sponsored by donor agencies which prefer to fund one large project than many smaller projects.

5.4 Tank System

Another alternative for irrigation method is Tank System. Tank irrigation is an old, established method in most of the semi-arid tropical parts of the country. It is a reservoir created by constructing earthen wall across the slope of a valley to store rain water. Tank irrigation systems are more economical. It is very much prevalent in both north India as well as in the south. It was a very popular method of irrigation before independence but after independence its control was transferred to Public Works Department of the state governments. Over the years, tank irrigation got marginalised because of different irrigation methods.

Oppen, in his intensive studies on tank irrigation suggests the creation of a Tank Irrigation Authority. Tanks can be easily constructed and maintained by involving local communities. He also suggests to lining the canals to reduce seepage losses. Oppen says that it is possible to make tank irrigation attractive in comparison to tubewells, through effective management. If managed properly tank irrigation can provide a sustainable method of irrigation.

5.5 Water Harvesting

Recently water harvesting has become the most popular alternative method of sustainable irrigation and water consumption. This method requires a rainwater catchment unit consisting of a catchment area where the rain falls down. The water is then transported to the storage reservoir. The catchment area and storage depend on the demand of water on the amount of rainfall the area receives. The basic idea behind rain water harvesting is that instead of allowing runoff to cause erosion, it should be collected for better crop production.

Water harvesting includes inducing and increasing runoff by using surface treatments and scheduling irrigation in scarcity areas at critical stages of crop growth. This technology attempts to minimize interception, evaporation and surface storage while maximizing the runoff through surface treatment which at times consists of merely shaping and smoothening out the top surface, thus providing the land slope. It also curbs soil erosion and results in better soil and water management.

Nirmal Sengupta emphasises on the traditional irrigation technologies and advocates for an ingenious way of water harvesting with the help of *ahars*. An *ahar* is a rectangular catchment basin, with embankments on three sides. The fourth side faces the catchment area. He points out that though most *ahars* are small, one can also find them with sides more than a kilometer long, irrigating more than a thousand acres of land. Water harvesting systems are environmentally sound as well as helpful in soil and water conservation. Centre for Science and Environment is playing a crucial role in popularizing rain water harvest in India. It is working like a supporting agency in many parts of the country with the help of other local organizations. Many schools, government offices are trying this method. Having tried it in the Delhi's Chief Minister's residence, Delhi government has now made rain water harvesting mandatory for every new house or hotel being built in the capital. 'The Delhi Development Authority and the Municipal Corporation of Delhi have made amendments in the existing building bylaws, making it compulsory for every house or hotel, which is 200 yards and more in area, to undertake rainwater harvesting'. [10] However, rain water harvesting is only part of the solution to the problems in semi-arid areas.

5.6 Canal Irrigation System

Canal Irrigation is another viable alternative in irrigation system. In north India canal irrigation system is very advanced and very helpful in irrigation. Nirmal Sengupta has analysed canal system in South Bihar. These canals are called *pynes*, which are led off from points facing the current of the local rivers to the agricultural lands. These are around 30 or 40 kilometers long, with many distributaries. It irrigates up to around hundred villages. *Pynes* system did not stop the river from flowing to its natural way as large dams do and so not cause serious ecological problems. Only the excess capacity of a river during the rains flowed into the canals. In some areas these canals filled up storage tanks that made irrigation possible after the rains.

Canal Irrigation System was very developed and popular in pre-British period. But gradually it started disappearing because of its inability to meet the increasing demand for hydro electricity. Today, when the ecological cost of large dams is so high, it would be worth reviving this project.

Many alternative irrigation technologies have been discussed above. These are also not without their drawbacks. But if planned properly and carefully, they can provide viable alternative irrigation methods that will be ecologically sustainable.

5.7 Alternative Hydro Power

The main reason behind the development and popularity of large dams are twin objectives of irrigation and hydropower generation. Small hydro electric technology is not given importance due to its inability to provide electricity for industrial and urban requirements.

The environmental groups which are pursuing alternate development model point out that small hydroelectric projects would provide electricity to rural areas to help develop local skills and resources. Since these projects are small in nature they do not cause submergence, displacement and other ecological hazards.

Small hydroelectric techniques are cheaper. It costs about Rs. 16,000 per kilowatt compared to Rs. 32,000 per kilowatt for conventional power. However, developmental aid agencies and international development banks who are the main sponsors for the large dams does not bother about this. 'World Bank lent $ 1.68 billion globally for large scale hydroelectric projects during 1976-80, as against nothing, for the development of small projects'. [11]

Unfortunately, most countries prefer to build large dams in order to meet the demands of heavy industry and to meet the urban requirement for electricity. On the contrary, 'Chinese have relied on indigenous labour, capital and technology to build small hydroelectric projects (SHP) in thousands, more than 88,000'. [12] In China they run small factories of chemical fertilizers, cement, agricultural machinery, rice, soap, leather and simple metal goods by SHP. SHP also provides an efficient option for producing electricity. It is estimated that 86 percent of rural residents' demands are met by SHP.

5.8 Conclusion

In India SHP is not given due importance because of the country's emphasis on industrialisation and urbanisation. But some mechanism should be developed and SHP should be made more popular because it is economically viable for a country like India and more environment friendly.

In this way, it has been tried to explore different alternative methods for irrigation and power generation for which large dams are constructed. An attempt is made to analyse irrigation in relation to two dominant ideas of today viz. Equity and sustainability. The dominant irrigation policy of large dams in India has proved inadequate on both these counts. Alternative irrigation methods are being evolved by the environmental and people's movements in India today which have emphasized sustainability and equitability as the principles for an alternative development model.

The main logic behind the opposition of the Swarn Rekha Dam, by the tribals is their notion of 'development'. For them large dams, modernisation, industrialisation and urbanisation are not the right steps of development. They perceive that they are marginalised because of this development. Their development is their present ecologically wise culture and ecologically respectful life which present an alternative vision of a sustainable world. According to them, over the centuries they have constantly fought an unequal battle against outside oppressors – the state and the market. Their fear is that their material base i.e. natural resources and their cultural autonomy are constantly being eroded.

The people of Swarn Rekha Andolan emphasise the creation of an alternative state structure – self-sufficient village rule – based on decentralization and participation of indigenous people, where Manaki Munda system and Willkinsion's rule should be followed. In their fight against the dams and imposed 'development' through government projects, they have been able to bring together many groups and ideologies, put them together in one platform. Their remarkably effectiveness had led to the postponement of the construction of Swarn Rekha dam.

Ganga Mukti Andolan primarily fought against the feudal system of 'Panidari' but in that process took up many other social, political and environmental issues. That helped the movement to broaden its base.

These two movements are examples of successful environmental movements at the grass root level. They remained local because they were led and represented by local people. When these movements were taking place in different parts of Bihar (and now Jharkhand), these issues were not even part of national intellectual discourse.

These two environmental movements based on completely two different environmental issues shows that the environment movement in third world countries (including India) are based on survival of the people. In the long span of struggle the (activists of GMA and Subernreha Andolan) took up many social, political and cultural issues also but their prime concern always had been their survival because these movements started with that. This is the finding of this research work and it proves the hypothesis with which the work had started.

The success of these movements provides a new vision of Indian state. For a stable and successful democracy, expectations and desires of the people must be taken case of.

These movements are providing a critique of the existing development model and a vision for a sustainable future that has been the focal point of every environment and social movement. They consider nature, land, forest and community as the ultimate factors for a happy, prosperous and just life. They believe in a harmonious relationship between human beings and nature.

Notes

1. Sudhir Chandra, To my successor, *The Times of India: Sunday Review*, 8th November 1987.
2. Ibid.

3. Atul Kohli, *The State and Poverty in India: The Politics of Reform*, Cambridge University Press, Cambridge, 1987.

4. Centre for Science and Environment, *The State of India's Environment 1984-85; The Second Citizens' Report, New Delhi, 1985*

5. Quoted in Amita Baviskar, *In the Belly of the River* Oxford University Press, Delhi, 1995.

6. Madhav Gadgil and Ramchandra Guha, *This Fissured Land: An Ecological History of India,* Oxford University Press, Delhi, 1992.

7. UNDP, United Natins Development Programme, Human Development Report, Oxford University Press, New York, 1992.

8. E.F. Schumacher, *Small is Beautifu* : *A study of Economics As If People Mattered,* Blond and Briggs, London, 1973.

9. As quoted in Darryl D'Monte, *Temple or Tombs?* New Delhi: Centre for Science and Environment 1985, p. 224.

10. *The Times of India,* 4th May 2001, New Delhi.

11. As quoted in Satyajit Singh, *Taming the Waters: The Political Economy of Large Dams in India,* Oxford University Press, New Delhi, 1997.

12. *Ibid*

Appendices

Appendix 1

National Conservation Strategy and Policy Statement on Environment and Development

(Ministry of Environment and Forest, Government of India, June 1992)

We are in the last decade of an extra-ordinarily eventful twentieth century. The world has seen spectacular political, social, cultural, economic and scientific progress during this century. But this progress has been monopolized by the chosen few at the unbelievably and indescribably large cost of the majority of mankind. The most disconcerting manifestation of this lop sided progress has been our planet's ravaged ecology.

A good environmental sense has been one of the fundamental features of India's ancient philosophy. However, during the last few decades global circumstances have forced our country into a situation where it is becoming increasingly difficult to practice a life style that does not push this planet towards doom. During the last ten years, there has been a gratifying resurgence of this good environmental sense in this country. The most important aspect of this growing environmental consciousness in this country is its permeation at the establishment as also the people's level.

It is imperative that environmental consciousness becomes a pre-occupation with our people as no amount of government intervention can reverse ecological collapse. I see clear signs of that happening in India. Against this backdrop, we now have a system of environmental checks and balances fully in place. There is enough institutional, legislative and political strength to combine with a responsive citizenry to produce a practicable environmental culture. In Constitutional terms too, India has enough guarantees to protect its ecological systems.

Since the inception of this Ministry, we have evolved enough to be able to chart out a life, which is happy without compromising the environment. There is a sizeable number of people who can rein in an indiscriminate establishment. In fact, we are now working towards a unique compatibility between the Development and the Environment.

We have our great past to draw from to create an equally great future. I see this environmentally degraded present only as an aberration for an enlightened civilization.

What you will read in the following pages are some of the specific means through which we propose to attain the goals of an environmentally wise society.

1.0 Preamble

1.1 The survival and well-being of a nation depend on sustainable development. It is a process of social and economic betterment that satisfies the needs and values of all interest groups without foreclosing future options. To this end, we must ensure that the demand on the environment from which we derive our sustenance, does not exceed its carrying capacity for the present as well as future generations.

1.2 In the past, we had a great tradition of environmental conservation which taught us to respect nature and to take cognizance of the fact that all forms of life - human, animal and plant - are closely interlined and that disturbance in one gives rise to an imbalance in other's. Even in modem times, as is evident in our constitutional provisions and environmental legislation and planning objectives, conscious efforts have been made for maintaining environmental security along with developmental advances. The Indian Constitution has laid a new important trail in the Section on Directive Principles of State Policy by assigning the duties for the State and all citizens through article 48 A and article 51 A(g) which state that the "State shall endeavour to protect and improve the environment and to safeguard the forests and wildlife in the country" and "to protect and improve the natural environment including forests, lakes and rivers and wildlife, and to have compassion for the living creatures".

1.3 Nevertheless, over the years, there has been progressive pressure on the environment and the natural resources, the alarming consequences of which are becoming evident in increasing proportions. These consequences detract from the gains of development and worsen the standard of living of the poor who are directly dependent on natural resources. It is in this context that we need to give a new thrust towards conservation and sustainable development.

1.4 The National Conservation Strategy and the Policy Statement on Environment and Development are in response to the need for laying down the guidelines that will help to weave environmental considerations into the fabric of our national life and of our development process. It is an expression of our commitment for reorienting policies and action in unison with the environmental perspective.

2.0 Environmental Problem: Nature and Dimensions

2.1 Environmental problems in India can be classified into two broad categories:

- those arising as negative effects of the very process of development; and
- those arising from conditions of poverty and under-development.

The first category has to do with the impact of efforts to achieve rapid economic growth and development and continuing pressures of demand generated by those sections of society who are economically more advanced and impose great strains on the supply of natural resources. Poorly planned developmental projects are also often environmentally destructive. The second category has to do with the impact on the health and integrity of our natural resources (land, soil, water, forests, wildlife, etc.) as a result of poverty and the inadequate availability, for a large section of our population, of the means to fulfil basic human needs (food, fuel, shelter, employment, etc.). Needless to say, the two problems are interrelated.

2.2 Population is an important resource for development, yet it is a major source of environmental degradation when it exceeds the threshold limits of the support systems. Unless the relationship between the multiplying population and life support systems can be stabilized, development programmes, however, innovative, are not likely to yield the desired results. It is possible to expand the "carrying capacity' through technological advances and spatial distribution. But neither of these can. support unlimited population growth. Although technological progress will add to the capabilities for sustaining a large number of population, the need for a vigorous drive for population control can hardly be over emphasized in view of the linkage between poverty, population growth and the environment.

2.3 Even today, over 250 million children, women and men suffer from under-nutrition. The scenario for the coming years is alarming and we are likely to face food crisis unless we are in a position to increase crop and animal productivity on a continuing basis, since the only option open to us for increasing production is productivity improvement Also, access to food will have to be ensured through opportunities for productive employment.

2.4 A growth in domesticated animal population has been accompanied by a loss of area under grasslands and pastures. Hardly, 3.5 per cent of our geographical area is under grasslands, while our domesticated animal population numbers nearly 500 million. The livelihood security of majority of our people depends on land and water based occupations such as crop and animal husbandry, forestry and fisheries.

2.5 Out of total area of India of about 329 million hectares, 175 million hectares of land require special treatment to restore such land to productive and profitable use. The degradation is caused by water and wind erosion (150 million ha), salinity and alkalinity (8 million ha) and river action and other factors (7 million ha).

2.6 Our forest wealth is dwindling due to over-grazing, over-exploitation both for commercial and house-hold needs, encroachments, unsustainable practices including certain practices of shifting cultivation and developmental activities such as roads, buildings, irrigation and power projects. The recorded forest cover in the country is 75.01 million ha which works out to 19.5 per cent of the total geographical area against the broad national goal of 33 per cent for the plain areas and 66 per cent for hilly regions. Even within this area, only 11 per cent constitute forests with 40 per cent or more of crown cover. According to the State of Forest Report, 1991, the actual forest cover in the country was 64.07 million hectares during 1987-89. The loss of habitat is leading to the extinction of plant, animal and microbial species. According to the Botanical and Zoological Surveys of India, over 1500 plant and animal species are in the, endangered category. The biological impoverishment of the country is a serious threat to sustainable advances in biological productivity. Gene erosion also erodes the prospects for deriving full economic and ecological benefits from recent advances in molecular biology and genetic engineering.

2.7 Our unique wetlands, rich in aquatic and bird life, providing food and shelter as also the breeding and spawning ground for the marine and fresh water fishes, are facing problems of pollution and over-exploitation. The major rivers of the country are also facing problems of pollution and siltation. Our long coastline is under similar stress. Our coastal areas have been severely damaged due to indiscriminate construction near the water-line. Coastal vegetation including mangroves and sea grasses is getting denuded. Our mountain ecosystems are under threat of serious degradation. Extensive deforestation leading to the erosion of valuable topsoil is threatening the livelihood security of millions of hill people. Equally serious is the downstream effects of the damage done upstream. Indo-gangetic agriculture, often described as a potential bread basket in the world, is being damaged beyond repair as a result of soil degradation. Some areas are facing problems of water-logging and rising water tables because of poorly planned and ill-executed irrigation. In other areas, the water table is receding because of over-exploitation of ground water. Furthermore, the quality of groundwater is being affected due to chemical pollution and in coastal areas, due to the ingress of sea water. The excessive use of fertilizers and pesticides impose threat to human health, to the genetic stocks and reduces the natural soil fertility in the long run. The absence of an integrated land and water use policy for the country is taking a heavy toll on these basic natural assets.

2.8 Coral reefs are the most productive marine ecosystems and provide habitat for diverse flora and fauna. These ecosystems are adversely affected by indiscriminate exploitation of coral for production of lime, recreational use and for ornamental trade. Similarly, the fragile environs of island ecosystems have been subjected to pressures of various forms including migration of people from the mainland.

2.9 Global atmospheric changes resulting in altered temperature and precipitation and rising ocean levels, are no longer within the realm of mere theoretical possibilities. Combination of local subsidence, greenhouse induced sea-level rise and coastal environmental degradation may lead to periodic floods, incursion of salt water, melting of glaciers and river flooding. Local changes of average rainfall will severely affect agriculture and water supply, especially in semi-arid areas.

2.10 Compounding these human-inflicted wounds on natural ecosystems and life-support mechanisms, we are facing serious problems of pollution and unsanitary conditions especially in urban areas. Pollution arising from toxic wastes and non-biodegradable consumer articles is tending to increase.

2.11 Lack of opportunities for gainful employment in villages and the ecological stresses is leading to an ever increasing movement of resource-poor families to towns. Mega cities are emerging and urban slums are expanding. Illiteracy and child labour are persisting. There has been a substantial urban growth in the last four decades. This has resulted in congestion and squatter settlements with millions of people having no access to the basic needs of civic amenities. The green cover in our urban centres has been largely destroyed and once beautiful garden cities have become concrete jungles. The man-made heritage in India has been often gravely and even irrevocably damaged.

2.12 A large number of industries and other development projects have been incorrectly sited, leading, on the one hand, to over-congestion and over-pollution in our urban centres and on the other hand, to diversion of population and economic resources from the rural areas. This has also resulted in the pollution of most of our water bodies which are major constituents of our life support systems. Pollution of water bodies, in turn, has adversely affected the growth of aquatic fauna and flora which is an environmentally undesirable phenomenon for any ecosystem. The problems of women in villages are compounded in this whole scenario of energy, environmental and developmental imbalance. The incidence on malaria is high in many parts of the country. Safe drinking water is still a luxury in many villages. Liver ailments and gastro-intestinal diseases are common due to unclean drinking water.

2.13 It is difficult to clearly delineate the causes and consequences of environmental degradation in terms of simple one-to-one relationships. The causes and effects are often interwoven in complex webs of social, technological and environmental factors. For instance, from a purely scientific and technological standpoint, soil erosion would result from the cultivation of marginal lands. However, from the point of view of a comprehensive environmental impact analysis, it is important to go further back and analyze the circumstances that force people to cultivate marginal lands. Viewed in this light, it becomes clear that a concern for the environment is essentially a desire to see that national development proceeds along rational, sustainable lines. Environmental conservation is, in fact, the very basis of all development.

2.14 The overriding impact of adverse demographic pressures on our resources and ecosystems due to poverty and overpopulation of man and livestock has to be highlighted. Unless there is a curb on population growth and even a reduction of such populations and a corresponding improvement in land use policies, the current trend of over-exploitation and ecological degradation is not likely to improve.

2.15 Thus, we are faced with the heed for accelerating the pace of development for alleviation of poverty which is, to a great extent, responsible for many of our environmental problems. On the other hand, we have to avoid proceeding along paths with environmental costs so high that these activities cannot be sustained. Development has to be sustainable and all round, whether for the poor or the not so-poor or for the village folk or for the town people. The development models followed so far need to be reviewed.

3.0 Actions Taken

In recognition of the felt need for environmental protection, various regulatory and promotional measures have been taken in our country over the past twenty years. These include the following

3.1 Legal

- The Wildlife (Protection) Act, 1972, amended in 1983, 1986 and 1991.
- The Water (Prevention and Control of Pollution) Act, 1974, amended in 1988.
- The Water'(Prevention and Control of Pollution) Cess, Act, 1977, amended in 1991.
- The Forest (Conservation) Act, 1980, amended in 1988.
- The Air (Prevention and Control of Pollution) Act, 1981, amended in 1988.
- The Environment (Protection) Act, 1986.
- The Motor Vehicle Act, 1938, amended in 1988.
- The Public Liability Insurance Act, 1991.
- A Notification on Coastal Regulation Zone, 1991.

3.2 Institutions

- Department of Environment in 1980 and the integrated Ministry of Environment & Forests in 1985, Department of Science and Technology, Department of Agriculture and Cooperation, Department of Biotechnology, Department of

Ocean Development, Department of Space, Department of Non-Conventional Energy Sources, Energy Management Centre, Council of Scientific and Industrial Research etc. at the Centre, Departments of Environment at the State and Union Territory level.

- Central Pollution Control Board and State Pollution Control Boards.
- Central Forestry Board.
- Indian Council of Forestry Research and Education with specialized institutions for research in and zone, forestry, moist and deciduous forests, wood technology, genetics and tree breeding and deciduous forests.
- Forest Survey of India (FSI) and the Wildlife Institute of India (VAI) in addition to the existing organizations like Botanical Survey of India (BSI) and Zoological Survey of India (ZSI).
- National Land-use and Wasteland Development Council.
- National Wastelands Development Board.
- Indian Board of Wildlife.
- National Museum of Natural History, Centre for Environmental Education, Institute for Himalayan Environment and Development and Centres of Excellence in specialized subject areas are among the various institutions set up.

3.3 Prevention and Control of Pollution

- Water and air quality monitoring stations in selected areas.
- Use-based zoning and classification of major rivers.
- Notification and enforcement of standards for polluting industries through the Central and State Pollution Control Boards.
- Rules for manufacture, storage, transportation and disposal of hazardous substances.
- On-site and off-site emergency plans for preparedness against chemical accidents.
- Fiscal incentives for installation of pollution control devices.

- Ganga Action Plan to prevent pollution of the river and restore its water quality which could be expanded to cover other major river systems subject to availability of resources.
- Identification of critically polluted areas and of highly polluting industries.

3.4 Conservation of Forests and Wildlife

- Adoption of a new Forest Policy (1988) with the principal aim of ensuring ecological balance through conservation of biological diversity, soil and water management, increase of tree cover, meeting the requirements of the rural and tribal population, increase in the productivity, efficient utilization of forest produce, substitution of wood and people's involvement for achieving these objectives.
- Under the Forest (Conservation) Act, 1980 stringent provisions for preventing diversion of forest land for any other purpose.
- Setting up of the National Wastelands Board to guide and oversee the wastelands development programme by adopting a mission approach for enlisting people's participation, harnessing the inputs of science and technology and achieving interdisciplinary coordination in programme planning and implementation.
- Formulation of a National Wildlife Action Plan.
- An exercise for preparation of a National Forestry Action Programme.
- Establishment of National Parks and Sanctuaries covering about 4% of the country's area.
- Eco-development plans for sanctuaries and National Parks.
- Identification of bio-geographical zones in the country for establishing a network of protected areas including seven Biosphere Reserves set up so far.
- Management Plans for identified wetlands, mangrove areas and coral reefs.
- Formulation of a National River Action Plan.

3.5 Land and Soil

- Surveys by the All India Soil, and Land-Use Survey Organization.
- Treatment of catchment in selected river valley projects and integrated watershed management projects in catchment of flood prone rivers.
- Assistance to States to control shifting cultivation.
- Assistance for reclamation and development of ravine areas.
- Drought prone areas programme.
- Desert development programme.

3.6 Environmental Impact Assessment

- Establishment of procedures for environmental impact assessment and clearance with regard to selected types of projects requiring approval of the Government of India.
- Prior clearance of projects requiring diversion of forests for non- forest purpose under the Forest (Conservation) Act 1980
- Formulation of Environmental guidelines for projects in various sectors.

3.7 Other Activities

- Eco-Task Forces of ex-servicemen for ecological restoration through afforestation and soil conservation.
- National Environmental Awareness Campaigns for creating environmental awareness through non-governmental organizations.
- Surveys and research studies.
- Training programmes, workshops and seminars for building up professional competence and for creation of awareness.

4.0 Constraints and Agenda for Action

4.1 The modest gains made by the steps taken during the past few years leave no room for complacency when viewed in the context of enormous challenges. We can meet the challenges only by redirecting the thrust of our developmental process so that the basic needs of our people are fulfilled by making judicious and sustainable use of our natural resources. Conservation, which covers a wide range of concerns and activities, is the key element of the policy for sustainable development. Framing a conservation strategy is, therefore, an imperative first step. Development requires the use and modification of natural resources; conservation ensures the sustainability of development for the present and in the future. The conservation strategy is to serve as a management guide for integrating environmental concerns with developmental imperatives.

4.2 The primary purpose of the strategy and the policy statement is to include & reinforce our traditional ethos and to build up a conservation society living in harmony with Nature and making frugal and efficient use of resources guided by the best available scientific knowledge.

4.3 The agenda for action in this regard will include the following

- to ensure sustainable and equitable use of resources for meeting the basic needs of the present and future generations without causing damage to the environment;
- to prevent and control future deterioration in land, water and air which constitute our life-support systems;
- to take steps for restoration of ecologically degraded areas and for environmental improvement in our rural and urban settlements;
- to prevent further damage to and conserve natural and man-made heritage;
- to ensure that development projects are correctly sited so as to minimize their adverse environmental consequences;
- to ensure that the environment and productivity of coastal areas and marine ecosystems are protected;
- to conserve and nurture the biological diversity, genepool and other resources through environmentally sustainable development and management of ecosystems, with special emphasis on our mountain, marine and coastal, desert, wetlands, riverine and island ecosystems; and,
- to protect the scenic landscapes, areas of geomorphological significance, unique and representative biomes and ecosystems and wildlife habitats, heritage sites/structures and areas of cultural heritage importance.

4.4 To address to the above stated agenda, the instruments for action will include the following:

- to carry out environmental impact assessment of all development projects right from the planning stage and integrate it with their cost-benefit considerations. Appropriate costs of environmental safeguards and regeneration would continue to form an integral part of the projects;
- to ensure that all projects above a certain size and in certain ecologically sensitive areas should require compulsory prior environmental clearance;
- to incorporate environmental safeguards and protection measures, in policies, planning, site selection, choice of technology and implementation of development projects like agriculture, water resource development, industry, mineral extraction and processing, energy, forestry, transport and human settlements;
- to encourage research, development and adoption of environmentally compatible technologies; and to promote application of the modern tools of science and technology for conservation, bridging of large gaps in supply and demand as well as control and monitoring of natural resources;
- to elicit and ensure participation of people in programmes for environmental improvement and for integrating the environmental concerns in planning and implementation of development programmes;
- to create environmental consciousness through education and mass awareness programmes;
- to aim at moderation of process of demand unleashed by the developmental process itself by taking measures to recycle waste materials and natural resources, conserve energy, conserve use of natural resources in industrial products by measures like wood substitution and generally try to reach moderation's in life styles consistent with sustainability and human dignity; to develop appropriate organizational structures and a pool of professional manpower to serve as the cadre for environmental management service; and,

- to effectively implement the various environmental laws and regulations for environmental protection through creation or strengthening of the requisite enforcement machinery.

5.0 Priorities and Strategies for Action

5.1 Population Control

5.1.1 Unabated population growth, as at present, not only adds to the economic burden for all developmental activities, but also reduces the impact of economic growth on our society. Therefore, for the success of our planning, population control becomes the most urgent necessity. A comprehensive programme, with strong political backing and appropriate socio-economic measures, fully utilizing the available scientific know-how, simultaneously making efforts for developing new methodologies, and supported by modern communication technology and managerial and organizational skills, is essential for success in this most difficult area. Population control should be a national mission for the next decade. Despite efforts of several years, population control projects have not met with success. More stern measures such as legislative and better incentives are needed.

5.1.2 Along with the development programmes to improve the living conditions, action must be directed towards stabilization of population including the following measures:

Launching a time bound national campaign for population stabilization with the small family as a socially responsible objective;

- Increased support for female education, female employment, and of social security programmes;
- Easier access to the means of family planning and health care facilities;
- Added incentives in terms of taxation and other benefits for family planning;
- Environmental sanitation, prevention and control of communicable diseases through integrated vector control and health education; and,

- Adoption of decentralized renewable energy devices that enhance quality of life in remote pockets while taking special care of the health needs of women.

5.2 Conservation of Natural Resources

5.2.1 Land and Water

5.2.1.1 An integrated land and water management approach is extremely important to sustain the food production, animal husbandry and other activities.

5.2.1.2 Amelioration of water-logged and salt affected lands, command area development, protection of good agricultural land against diversion to urban and other uses, prevention of land fragmentation, maintenance of sustained productivity of soil and conservation of lands with forests and vegetal cover are the integral components of sustainable management.,

5.2.1.3 The importance of water as a finite, though a renewable resource, must be clearly recognized. Land and water use are to be considered together, particularly in the context of recurring droughts and floods. Water conservation measures; discipline on use of water; economizing the consumption of water in households, agriculture and industry; and appropriate recycling would be essential.

5.2.1.4 The steps to be taken for sustainable use of land and water should include the following:

- Classification, zoning and apportionment of land for designated uses such as, agriculture, forestry, grassland, green areas, industrial activities, catchment areas and watersheds and human settlements based on assessment of their capabilities and environmental considerations;
- Enactment of laws for appropriate land uses to protect the soil from erosion, pollution and degradation;
- Protection of land near water bodies and prevention of construction there upon;
- Measures to ensure equitable access to and responsibility for sustainable use of land and water resources;
- Micro-level planning to develop appropriate methodology and implementation of action plan by involving the people at the

village level in social forestry programmes, land use planning, afforestation etc.;

- Countrywide campaign to minimize soil and run-off losses by carrying out extensive works like contour trenching, contour bounding, terracing, construction of small storages, catchment treatment and protection of the vegetal cover in the catchments and watersheds. This is to be a specific charge of project authorities in all irrigation, power, road and agricultural projects;
- Restoration and reclamation of degraded areas including weed infested areas, mined areas, grazing lands and salt affected soils;
- Measures for preventing wind erosion by undertaking special programmes of conservation and afforestation in desert areas;
- Development of suitable agro-silvipastoral techniques with special emphasis on hilly areas and in, and semi-arid zones;
- Building up a network for assessment and monitoring of soil and water (surface and ground water) quality throughout, the country which should be on a permanent basis as in the case of meteorological stations;
- Measures for water conservation, recycling and optimal conjunctive use of surface and ground water for specific uses;
- Legislative measures to check over-exploitation of surface and ground water for various uses;
- Conservation of wetlands for ensuring sustainable ecological and economic benefits;
- Encouragement to and improvement in traditional methods of rain water harvesting and storage.
- Stringent measures for prevention and control of pollution due to indiscriminate disposal of solid wastes,, effluents and hazardous substances in land and water courses;
- Control and abatement of pollution of water bodies from municipal and industrial wastes generated from urban habitats by intercepting and diverting such wastes away from water bodies;

- Classification, zoning and regulations for maintaining the quality of the water bodies to protect and enhance their capabilities to support the various designated uses; and,
- Adoption of low cost sanitation technology for prevention and control of pollution in water courses.

5.2.2 Atmosphere

5.2.2.1 For prevention and control of atmospheric pollution including noise pollution, the thrust will be on the following:

- Use of clean fuels and clean technologies, energy efficient devices and air and noise pollution control systems;
- Setting up of source specific and area wise air quality standards and time bound plans to prevent and control pollution;
- Proper location of projects to minimize the adverse impact on people and environment;
- Incentives for environmentally benign substitutes, technologies and energy conservation;
- Raising of green belts with pollution tolerant species;
- Developing coping mechanisms for future climatic changes as a result of increased emission of carbon dioxide and greenhouse gases; and
- Appropriate action to control adverse impact on Indian continent due to ozone depletion and other gaseous effects in the atmosphere at global level.

5.2.3 Biodiversity

5.2.3.1 About 90 per cent of the world food comes from 20 plant species. The plant breeders find that they have to turn more and more to the wild species to introduce into the cultivated forms desired qualities of resistance to pests and diseases and the ability to withstand adverse soil and weather conditions. India's biological diversity is very rich but unfortunately its wealth is being eroded due to various reasons. This diversity needs to be preserved and the immediate task will be to devise and enforce time bound plans for saving the endangered plant and animal species as well as habitats of biological resources. Action for conservation must be directed to:

- Intensification of surveys and inventorisation of biological resources in different parts of the country including the island ecosystems. The survey should include information on distribution pattern of particular species, population and communities and the status of ethnobiologically important groups;
- Conservation of biodiversity through a network of protected areas including Biosphere Reserves, Marine Reserves, National Parks, Sanctuaries, Gene Conservation Centres, Wetlands, Coral Reefs and such other natural habitats of biodiversity. This should include taxonomic and ecological studies on the flora and fauna with adequate emphasis placed on the lower vertebrate, invertebrate and micro-flora which are important in contributing to the healthy maintenance of ecosystems;
- Full and correct rehabilitation of rural poor/tribals displaced due to creation of national parks/biosphere reserves/tiger reserves;
- Conservation of micro-fauna and micro-flora which help in reclamation of wastelands and revival of biological potential of the land;
- Protection and sustainable use of plant and animal genetic resources through appropriate laws and practices;
- Protection of domesticated species/varieties of plants and animals in order to conserve indigenous genetic diversity;
- Maintenance of corridors between national parks, sanctuaries, forests and other protected areas;
- Emulation and support for protecting traditional skills and knowledge for conservation;
- Development of methodologies to multiply, breed and conserve the threatened and endangered species through modern techniques of tissue culture and biotechnology;
- Discouragement of monoculture and plantation of dominating and exotic species, in areas unsuited for them and without sufficient experimentation; and,

- Restriction on introduction of exotic species of animals without adequate investigations.

5.2.4 Biomass

5.2.4.1 For the vast majority of our rural people, the foremost need is for fuel wood, timber, fodder, fibre, etc. The issue of sustainable resource utilization, therefore, has to be specially addressed first from the point of view of the biomass requirements of the rural poor. Action must be directed to:

- Devising ways and means by which local people can conserve and use thereafter the resources of the common lands and degraded forests, so that they have a stake in the continuing productivity of the resources;
- Encouraging private individuals and institutions to regenerate and develop their wastelands;
- Raising of fuel-wood species and provision of alternatives to reduce dependence on fuel-wood;
- Taking measures to increase the production of fodder and grasses to bridge the wide gap between supply and demand;
- Raising of bamboo and species providing small timber for local house-construction and agricultural implements;
- Increasing biomass to meet essential requirement of biomass based industry;
- Promoting direct relationship between forest-based industry and farmers to raise needed raw materials, provided this does not result in diversion of prime agricultural lands and displacement of small and marginal farmers;
- Extensive research and development in forestry for better regeneration and improved productivity;
- Development of technologies for enhancing the productivity and efficiency of use of all biomass resources (both terrestrial and marine);
- Institutional and technological systems to enable rural artisans to sustain biomass based crafts; and,
- Curtailment of the supply of subsidized biomass based resources to industrial consumers.

6.0 Development Policies from Environmental Perspectives

Implementation of the aims and objectives of conservation and sustainable development will require integration and internalization of environmental considerations in the policies and programmes of development in various sectors.

Curtailment of consumerism and shift towards use of environment friendly products and processes, and low waste generating technologies through conscious efforts and appropriate economic policies including pricing of natural resources as well as fiscal incentives and disincentives will be the guiding factors for ensuring conservation and sustainable development.

For environmental conservation and sustainable development, the steps which need to be taken in some of the key sectors of development activities are outlined in the following sections

6.1 Agriculture and Irrigation

For sustainable management of agriculture and irrigation, the action points should include the following:

6.1.1 Agriculture

- Development of pesticides and insecticides policy for the country;
- Development of integrated pest management and nutrient supply system;
- Development and promotion of methods of sustainable farming, especially organic and natural farming;
- Efficient use of inputs including agro-chemicals with minimal degradation of environment;
- Phasing out and stoppage of persistent and toxic pesticides and their substitution by environmentally safe and appropriate pesticides;
- Promotion of environmentally compatible cropping practices, bio-fertilisers and biopesticides;
- Restriction on diversion of prime agricultural land for other purposes;
- Ensuring land for different uses based upon land capability and land productivity;

- Evolving cost effective and efficient methods of water conservation and use;
- Incentives for cultivation of crops with high nutritive value and those with lesser demands on water and energy inputs;
- Encouraging crop rotation patterns;
- Strengthening of local bodies like Zilla Parishads, Panchayats and Samitis to ensure effective decentralization and optimal resource management; and,
- Anticipatory programmes and contingency plans for disasters such as drought, flood and climate change.

6.1.2 Irrigation

- Priority to small projects to meet the requirements of irrigation without causing significant alteration in the environmental conditions;
- Revival of traditional water management systems and development of alternate irrigation systems such as harvesting and conservation of run-off rain water;
- Measures for increasing the efficiency of water-use, water conservation and recycling;
- Measures for provision of drainage as an integral component of irrigation projects and to prevent water logging and leaching;
- Watershed management through catchment treatment of the drainage areas, protection of vegetal cover and measures to prevent siltation in an integrated manner with the irrigation authorities being fully accountable; catchment treatment would be so designed as to have a direct impact on the life of the reservoir, hydrological regime and life support systems. It would depend on the location specific conditions in each case;
- Adoption of command area development approach for all irrigation projects to ensure optimal utilization;
- Critical assessment of irrigation projects and delivery systems to ensure optimal utilization of water resources along with measures to mitigate environmental and social damage;
- Focus on decentralized network of small irrigation and water projects with minimum environmental disruption which will

be of great value to local communities and yet capable of generating surplus for other areas at low cost;

- Design and implementation of irrigation projects which are environmentally sustainable, based on lessons learnt from a critical analysis of all past projects; and,
- Continuous and ongoing evaluation and monitoring of all projects.

6.2 Animal Husbandry

The activities relating to animal husbandry should concentrate on the following:

- Development of an animal husbandry policy for the country;
- Intensification of sterilization programme for containing unsustainable growth in livestock population;
- Improvement in genetic variability of indigenous population;
- Distribution of animals like goats under the Integrated Rural Development Programme strictly consistent with the availability of pasture lands to reduce pressure on the lands;
- Propagation of wildlife and wildlife resources management on sustainable basis;
- Selective breeding of animals used for draught power to conserve fuel;
- Promotion of stall feeding and rotational grazing;
- Restoration and protection of grazing lands;
- Involvement of local people in the policy planning on pasture lands and stall feeding to avoid fodder scarcity; and,
- Incentive for growing fodder crops and establishment of fodder banks.

6.3 Forestry

Concerted efforts should be made for raising the forest cover and for conservation of existing forests which constitute an essential life support system and an important source of food, fibre, fodder, fuel and medicines etc. For attaining the goal of having at least one third of our land area under forest cover, intensified measures on a mission mode are required to be taken along with commensurate mobilization of resources for this purpose. As outlined in the National Forest Policy (1988), the action points should include the following:

- Maintenance of environmental stability through preservation and, where necessary, restoration of the ecological balance that has been adversely disturbed by serious depletion of the forests of the country;
- Conserving the natural heritage of the country by preserving the remaining natural forests with the vast majority of flora and fauna, which represent the biological diversity and genetic resources of the country;
- increasing substantially the forest/tree cover in the country through massive afforestation and social forestry programmes, especially on all denuded, degraded and unproductive lands involving the local people in this endeavour by giving them tangible economic motives and employment opportunities;
- Meeting the rights and concessions for requirements of fuel wood, fodder, minor forest produce and small timber of the rural and tribal population with due cognizance of the carrying capacity of forests;
- Increasing the productivity of forests to meet the essential national needs;
- Encouraging efficient utilization of forest produce;
- Restriction on diversion of forest lands for non-forest uses and compensatory afforestation in case where diversion is unavoidable;
- Afforestation on common lands by the local communities through usufruct-sharing schemes;
- Motivation of farmers/land owners to resort to tree farming in similar manner of crop based farming;
- Substitution of wood by other materials, alternative sources of energy and fuel efficient stoves;
- Permission to forest-based enterprises after a thorough scrutiny regarding the availability of raw materials;
- Supply of forest produce to the industrial consumers only at its true market value and not at concessional prices;

- Involvement of local people and dedicated grass roots nongovernmental organizations, in the afforestation programme and for protection of existing forests; and,
- Creation of land banks for compensatory afforestation.

6.4 Energy Generation and Use

For prevention and control of pollution and environmental hazards in energy generation and use as also for encouraging popularization of environmentally benign energy systems, the following measures should be taken:

- Environmental impact assessment prior to investment decisions and site selection; choice of practicable clean technologies for energy production and processes including waste utilization, treatment and disposal of solid wastes, effluents and emissions;
- Location of energy generation projects based on environmental considerations including pollution, displacement of people and loss of biodiversity;
- Decentralized small projects for meeting the rural energy needs and incentives for use of non-conventional energy sources;
- Incentives and punitive measures (including proper pricing) to prevent abuse and to promote the use of energy efficient devices in the production and distribution systems and for energy conservation in all sectors including households, agriculture, industry, power and transportation;
- Concerted efforts for development and propagation of non-conventional renewable energy generation systems; and,
- Setting up of biogas plants based on cow-dung, human excreta and vegetable wastes.

6.5 Industrial Development

Environmental considerations should be integrated while encouraging industrial growth. The action points in this regard should include a mix of promotional and regulatory steps which are as follows:

- Incentives for environmentally clean technologies, recycling and reuse of wastes and conservation of natural resources;

- Operationalisation of 'polluter pays principle' by introducing effluent tax, resource cess for industry and implementation of standards based on resource consumption and production capacity;
- Fiscal incentives to small-scale industries for pollution control and for reduction of wastes;
- While deciding upon sites, priority to compatible industries so that, to the extent possible, wastes from one could be used as raw material for the other and thus the net pollution load is minimized;
- Location of industries as per environmental guidelines for sitting of industry;
- Enforcement of pollution control norms in various types of industrial units depending on their production processes, technologies and pollution potential; particular attention to be paid to highly polluting industries;
- Encouragement for use of environmentally benign automobiles/motor vehicles and reduction of auto-emissions;
- Collective efforts for installation and operation of common effluent treatment facilities in industrial estates and in areas with a cluster of industries;
- Introduction of 'Environmental Audit' and reports thereof to focus on environment related policies, operations and activities in industrial concerns with specific reference to pollution control and waste management;
- Dissemination of information for public awareness on environmental safety aspects and stringent measures to ensure safety of workers and general population against hazardous substances and processes;
- Preparation of on-site emergency plans for hazardous industries and off-site emergency plans for districts in which hazardous units are located;
- Public liability insurance against loss or injury to life or property;

- Setting up of environment cells in industries for implementing environmental management plans and for compliance of the requisites of environmental laws;
- Internalizing the environmental safeguards as integral component of the total project cost;
- Environmental impact assessment from the planning stage and selection of sites for location of industries; and,
- Clearance by Ministry of Environment and Forests of all projects above a certain size and in certain fragile areas.

6.6 Mining and Quarrying

To prevent and to mitigate environmental repercussions in mining and quarrying operations, action must be directed to:

- Mined area rehabilitation and implementation of the environmental management plans concurrently with the on-going mining operations to ensure adequate ecological restoration of the affected areas;
- Rehabilitation of the abandoned mined areas in a phased manner so that scarce land resources can be brought back under productive use;
- Laying down of requisite stipulations for mining leases regarding tenure, size, shape and disposition with reference to geological boundaries and other mining conditions to ensure systematic extraction of minerals along with environmental conservation;
- Emphasis on production of value added finished products from mining so as to reduce indiscriminate extraction;
- Upgradation and beneficiation of minerals at the source, to the extent possible in order to ensure utilization of low-grade mineral resources and to reduce the cost of transportation, processing and utilization;
- Environmentally safe disposal of the by-products of mining;
- Restriction on mining and quarrying activities in sensitive areas such as hill slopes, areas of natural springs and areas rich in biological diversity;
- Discouraging selective mining of high grade ores and recovery of associated lower grade ores during mining; and,

- Environmental impact assessment prior to selection of sites for mining and quarrying activities.

6.7 Tourism

- To ensure sustainable growth of tourism without causing irreversible damage to the natural environment, activities relating to tourism should take care of the following :
- Promotion of tourism based on careful assessment of the carrying capacity and support facilities such as transport, fuel, water and sanitation;
- Development of tourism in harmony with the environmental conditions and without affecting the lifestyles of local people; and,
- Restriction on indiscriminate growth of tourism and strict regulation of the tourist activities in sensitive areas such as hill slopes, islands, coastal stretches, National Parks and Sanctuaries.

6.8 Transportation

- For prevention of pollution and for development of environmentally compatible transportation systems, the following steps should be taken :
- Improvement in mass transport system to reduce increasing consumption t of fuel, traffic congestion and pollution;
- Improved transport system based on bio-energy and other non-polluting energy sources;
- Rail transport and pipeline transport instead of road transport, where ever possible, by appropriate freight pricing so as to reduce congestion, fuel consumption and environmental hazards;,
- Transportation of hazardous substances through pipelines;
- Improvement in traffic flow through proper maintenance of roads, updated traffic regulation and strict enforcement of prescribed standards;
- Enforcement of smoke emission standards for containing vehicular exhausts, at the manufacturer and user level;
- Phasing out the use of lead in motor spirit; and,

- Regulations for environmental safety in transportation of hazardous substances.

6.9 Human Settlements

- To check unplanned growth of human settlements and to ensure a better quality of life for the rural and urban population, the action points should include the following :
- Creation of gainful employment opportunities and provision for meeting the basic needs through better communications, entertainment, medical and educational facilities in rural areas to check rural-urban migration;
- Decentralization of urbanization through establishment of secondary cities and towns with requisite infra-structural services and employment opportunities by developing human settlement perspective plan at national and state level;
- Disincentives for industrial and job location in existing urban centres which have exceeded their carrying capacity;
- Improvement of infra-structural facilities such as water supply, sewerage, solid waste disposal, energy recovery systems and transportation in an integrated manner;
- Promoting the use of indigenous building materials and appropriate construction technologies by revising building and planning codes supporting small scale production, skill upgradation of artisans and people oriented delivery systems;
- Conservation of heritage sites and buildings, through regulation to ensure that these are not demolished, encroached upon and affected by indiscriminate construction and pollution;
- Stock-taking of buildings, areas, monuments of heritage value in the country;
- Recycling of existing building stock to save green open compounds and save building material;
- Planning of shade giving and fruit bearing and ornamental trees along the road side, in the compounds of schools, hospitals, Government as well as private office buildings, places of worship, places meant for public fairs, assemblies

and markets, and the periphery of play grounds and water bodies;

- Botanical gardens representing the local flora;
- Raising of gardens, parks and open spaces in the towns and cities for public use and for promotion of environmental consciousness;
- Laying down a system for the propagation and protection of urban forestry by assigning responsibility amongst the various authorities;
- Deterrent measures to discourage indiscriminate growth of human settlement and polluting industries in vulnerable areas such as hilly regions and coastal stretches;
- Environmental appraisal of projects related to urban development and regional planning, preparation of environmental/eco-development plans for sensitive regions and sub-regions for evolving desirable norms and space standards;
- Prevention of environmental health problems and associated communicable and non-communicable diseases by educating people on personal hygiene, sanitation and use of potable water;
- Creation/ strengthening of health care facilities for all sections of society both in rural and urban areas; and,
- Establishment of monitoring systems and epidemiological data to ensure adequate early warning system for prevention and control of diseases.

7.0 International Cooperation

7.1 A major threat to sustainable development has been visualized, in recent years, from environmental problems of a global nature-ozone layer depletion, global warming and climate change, destruction of biological diversity, trans-boundary air pollution, marine pollution and land-based marine pollution, trans-boundary movement of hazardous 'substances. On a philosophical plain, the scientific proof of such problems provides an opportunity to reconsider the development path ushered in by the industrial revolution, and the blinkered pursuit of lifestyles which place extreme pressures on the natural resource base. But at a practical level, it means pressures on developing countries to take measures which they can ill-afford.

7.2 It has been India's firm conviction that it is the process of industrialization, and the continued profligacy of industrialized economies that have created the problems which threaten our planet and its life forms. Not only do they use up non-renewable natural resources in disproportionate quantities, but create discharges and emissions which disturb delicate balances in eco-systems and atmospheric equilibrium. It is true, of course, that this has not ' been done consciously or intentionally (except in matters such as dumping of hazardous wastes, or the use of nuclear and chemical weapons). Nevertheless, the responsibility is clearly established, as also the need for urgent and effective action, by the developed world, to prevent global disaster. This includes not only direct action, but also indirect measures such as creation of an economic order which helps developing countries to exert less pressure on their own natural resources.

7.3 The Indian approach to global environmental problems is generally in keeping with other developing countries and has the following basic elements:

- Our economic development cannot be hampered in the name of the global environment, which we have done nothing to damage and can do little to save. Our resources are required to meet our developmental needs such as education, nutrition, health services, drinking water, housing, sanitation, agriculture, industry, infrastructure, even all of which we find it difficult to provide having been behind in the race for development. Without this development, threats to the environment will in any case grow. In the short run, this developmental effort could even add to the discharges and emissions which cause global problems - but these are miniscule compared to the quantities which industrialized countries have already contributed. In any case, such emissions etc., can easily be compensated for a marginal reduction of the same in the industrialized world;

- For environmental protection and improvement, we will do our best with the resources available in the country. With new and additional funding support and transfer of environmentally sound technologies from the developed countries, we will be in a position to augment our capacity to deal with the environmental problems; and,
- Regulatory international regimes can be useful in some areas such as ozone depletion or even climate change - provided the special situation of developing countries is fully addressed. But in other sectors - such as forestry - such a regime is neither workable nor acceptable. In such sectors, what is required is a reduction of international economic and commercial pressures which generate unsustainable exploitation, and additional financial resources to tackle the damage already done.

7.4 India's traditional lifestyle still followed by a vast majority of its population :-- has always emphasized conservation of plant and animal life, waste minimization, recycling, simplicity in food habits and other such environment - friendly attitudes. There is no doubt that with economic development will also come lifestyles which require more intensive resource use. On the one hand we have to minimize the adverse environmental impacts of development (e.g., through legislation and control, impact assessment and monitoring, education and awareness). On the other, we have to continuously see how far the traditional Indian ethos can be reflected in modern lifestyles. If these efforts are supported by adequate financial resources from the international community, as well as the transfer (and development) of environmentally sound technology, India can contribute significantly to the international action to deal with global environmental problems.

8.0 Support Policies and Systems

Implementation of the aims and objectives of environmental policy will need support policies and systems for filling up of the gaps in the existing institutional set up, legislative instruments and enforcement mechanisms, research and development, mobilization of financial resources, creation of public awareness and training of professionals.

8.1 Strengthening of Institutions and Legislation

8.1.1 It will require strengthening of existing institutions at different levels. It will need a close linkage among the compartmentalized sectors which have been historically dealt with by separate organizations. It will call for a change in the institutional - mechanism for enlisting public participation. It will necessitate quick decision making on development projects based on assessment of their potential of rendering long term sustainable benefits to the society at large, particularly vulnerable sections. It will also require effective implementation of laws and regulations for environmental protection through strengthening of and closer interaction among the regulatory bodies and administrative machinery.

8.1.2 Existing laws and enforcement mechanisms should be subjected to periodic review to evaluate their adequacy and efficacy in the light of changed circumstances and experience.

8.2 Natural Resource Accounting

8.2.1 As economic policies form the frame-work for a range of sectoral development, it will be necessary to consider how these policies affect the quality and productivity of environmen6l resources. This will require a system of resource accounting along with the other exercises of cost benefit analyses.

8.2.2 In essence, indicators of growth such as GNP and GDP should include a measure of depletion cost and value judgments in terms of environmental resources. It will require instruments and expertise for evaluation and conscious trade offs, where unavoidable, to meet the legitimate development needs.

8.2.3 The Government will prepare, each year, a natural resources budget which will reflect the state and availability of resources like land, forests, water etc. and which will rationally allocate. these resources in keeping with the principles of conservation and sustainable development.

8.3 Training and Orientation Programmes

8.3.1 Available management resources in the enterprises/projects would be oriented towards environmental considerations and expertise to be developed through appropriate training programmes.

8.3.2 Formal education and training programme in specialized areas of pollution control and environmental management will be a continuing need. For this purpose, intensive programmes for education and training will need to be introduced in the universities, IITs and other professional institutions. Environmental education at the school level including training of teachers shall be an important component of educational programmes.

8.4 Promoting Environmental Awareness

To raise public awareness and involvement in environmental activities, the mass media ranging from local folklores to electronic media should serve as a vital role. To raise public awareness on environmental issues and to promote people's participation, in environmental activities and conservation of natural resources, development of environmental education resource material and use of traditional and modem media of communication need to be strengthened. Scope and functions of the existing environmental education centres should be further strengthened and enlarged to develop a network of infrastructure for environmental education including development of orientation centres and provision of educational material for visitors at the national parks, sanctuaries and tiger reserves.

8.5 Promoting Appropriate Environmental Technologies

Existing research and development efforts need to be strengthened to develop the appropriate low cost technologies considering the possibilities, opened up by biotechnology, genetic engineering, information and material technologies and remote sensing, tailored to the local environmental conditions.

8.6 Rehabilitation of Project Oustees

8.6.1 While implementing the projects in various sectors, conscious efforts should be made to avoid displacement of local people. Where it is unavoidable, necessary measures should be taken to ensure their rehabilitation by providing suitable facilities.

8.6.2 The Government will formulate a comprehensive national rehabilitation policy which, apart from other things, ensures that the oustees are economically better off than before and above poverty line as a result of their rehabilitation.

8.7 Role of Non-Governmental Organizations

8.7.1 Implementation of the conservation strategy would be impossible without active participation of the people. Non-Governmental Organizations (NGOs) can play an important role in mobilizing the people at grassroots. This will need a network among NGOs and interface between people and Government to work on community involvement, providing information on environmental surveillance and monitoring, transmitting development in science and appropriate technology to the people at large.

8.7.2 Environmental Information Centres should be set up at the district level to generate knowledge regarding traditional and endogenous system management practices. NGOs at the district level should be involved in the management and dissemination of the environmental information.

8.7.3 Non-Governmental Organizations, citizen groups and village level institutions like forests panchayats, and Gram Sabtra should be empowered with locus standi and. support for mobilization of public opinion and participation in development activities.

8.7.4 Managerial capacity of the NGOs should be strengthened. Training programmes for NGOs on regional basis should be organized. An advisory cell for rural NGOs should be made available at all district headquarters.

8.8 Women and Environment

Women at the grassroots level should be actively involved in the conservation programmes which should be income generating and self financing and sustainable on a long term basis and the Government Ministries/Departments should have an NGOs cell or at least Liaison Officer for interaction with the NGOs.

8.9 Partnership role of Centre and State Governments

Effective implementation of necessary measures, as outlined in the Statement, will be facilitated by a partnership role of Central and State Governments. Many environmental problems assume national significance. Hence, the policies and programmes at the State and Central level should be drawn up keeping in view overall national policy considerations. A monitoring mechanism involving central and state Government representatives will be set up for inter-action as required for implementation of the policy initiatives.

9.0 Conclusion

9.1 It is only through such initiatives the contours of which have been highlighted in preceding paragraphs, we will be in a position to resolve the conflicts which often arise between the environmental concerns and developmental pursuits that have a direct bearing on the very fabric of our society and life styles.

9.2 The task before us would be daunting if it were not for the many positive factors that are emerging: people's movements to conserve their own environment, greater public and media concern for environmental issues and spread of environmental awareness among children and youth.

9.3 It is up to us, as State and citizens, to undertake development pr6cess in keeping with our heritage and the traditional conservation ethos and in harmony with the environmental imperatives of this land.

Appendix 2

Environmental Guidelines Issued by the Ministry of Environment and Forests, Government of India

Hazardous Waste Management Guidelines

Guidelines for Occupier/Generator of Hazardous Wastes

In order to have a proper control over hazardous waste management, the regulatory authorities should specify the occupier or generator of hazardous waste:

1. To keep a complete record of the types, quantities and characteristics of hazardous waste.
2. To segregate hazardous waste at source from non-hazardous waste.
3. To transport hazardous waste only through the specified and registered transporters.
4. To fulfil the pre-transport requirements before transporting hazardous waste.
5. To dispose of hazardous waste only at the notified disposable facilities.
6. The regulatory authorities shall ask the occupier or generator to submit quarterly reports.
7. The authorities should ensure that the occupier/generator sends a copy of the manifest to them as soon as the hazardous wastes is shipped for ultimate disposal.
8. The regulatory authorities may allow the occupier/generator to store his hazardous waste on-site provided that:

- The waste is stored in the specified containers and occupier/generator follows the requirements for storing in the containers.
- The date upon which each period of storage begins is clearly marked and visible on each container.

- While being stored on-site, each container is labelled or marked with the words "HAZARDOUS WASTE" , both in English and respective local language.

9. The regulatory authorities may allow the occupier/generator to store his hazardous waste on-site a maximum quantity of 10,000 kgs or a truckload whichever is less for a maximum period of 90 days.
10. If an occupier/generator generates less than 1,000 kgs of hazardous waste in a month, he may be considered as a small quantity generator. Such type of generators may be allowed to store their waste on-site for a maximum period of 180 days. In any case, the quantity of waste should not exceed 6,000 kgs at any given point of time.
11. The regulatory authorities may provide an extension in the storage period to the occupier, on case-by-case basis, provided that:
12. An occupier/generator who generates less than 1000 kgs of hazardous waste in a month and who transports his waste more than a distance of 500 kms for off-site storage, treatment and/or disposal may be allowed to store hazardous waste on-site for a maximum period of 270 days at the discretion of regulatory authorities. In any case the quantity of waste should not exceed 10,000 kgs at any given point of time.
13. To ensure that the occupier/generator disposes their waste only in the notified disposal facilities.
14. In case of any unforeseen, temporary, and uncontrollable circumstances, the regulatory authorities may grant an extension to 90-day or 180-day or 270-day in the on-site period up to a maximum period of 30 days, after receiving written application from the occupier/generator.
15. An occupier/generator who generates less than 1000 kgs of hazardous waste more than 10,000 kgs or store hazardous waste more than 90 days or 180 days or 270 days, as the case may be, should be considered as an operator of a storage facility, unless an extension has been provided by the regulatory authorities.

16. An occupier may be allowed to store not more than one day's quantity of semi-solid hazardous waste at a time in containers near the source/point of generation, which is under the control of the operator generating the waste. In any case, the container should have marking of the words "HAZARDOUS WASTE" both in English and respective local language.
17. At all times there must be at least one employee either on the premises or on call with the responsibilities for co-ordinating all emergency response measures.
18. To inspect the on-site storage areas for proper storage.
19. In order to track the hazardous waste from the source of generation to the final disposal points, the regulatory authorities should introduce the manifest system. This system should not only help the regulatory authorities in tracking the hazardous waste but also ensure the safe disposal of the waste. The manifest system would serve as a "chain of custody" document. Every time the shipment changes hands, the responsible persons sign the manifest.

Guidelines for Transportation of Hazardous Waste

1. Transportation of hazardous waste being the important link in hazardous waste management system, it requires precise control to ensure safe disposal of such wastes. Therefore, it would be prudent to consider registering the transporters of hazardous waste with the Department of Environment & Forests in addition to the Department of Transport. This would enable the Ministry of Environment and Forests/respective State Pollution Control Boards to ensure safe and secured transport of hazardous wastes.
2. To ensure that the occupier/generator transport their hazardous waste only in the specified transport vehicles.
3. The transporters should be asked to train the drivers and helpers of hazardous waste transport vehicles to handle the wastes under emergency situations.

Guidelines for Owner/Operator of Hazardous Waste Storage, Treatment and Disposal Facility

1. Licensing system: The regulatory authorities may issue consent to an owner/operator of a facility who can demonstrate his technical, financial and managerial competence, and that his staff are properly trained. The authorities shall specify in the consent, the wastes which a facility can receive, the operational conditions which must be met, the monitoring and control procedures to be carried out and the records which must be kept. Along with the application for consent, the following information should be furnished by the owner/operator of a facility:

- Area required for the facility.
- Types of wastes to be handled, stored, treated and/or disposed.
- Facilities available for managing these wastes.
- Environment Impact Assessment of the area where the activity has been proposed.
- Contingency plan of the facility.

The regulatory authorities should ensure that the owner/operator of a facility has all necessary equipments such as fire control equipment, decontamination equipment, water spray system and internal communication or alarm systems capable of meeting any emergency situation at the facility.

2. Establishment of standards: The regulatory authorities should identify the Principal Organic Hazardous Constituents (POHC) in the waste and fix up standards for stack emission for POHC from the incinerator.

Also the effluent and ground water quality should be monitored regularly. The records of the facility should be checked regularly.

3. Post-closure care and use of property: The post closure-care for each hazardous waste storage, treatment, and/or disposal facility should begin after closure of the facility and the regulatory authorities must ensure that the post closure continues for 30 days from the date of closure. The local or

State Administrative body should be made responsible for the post-closure care.

4. To ensure that the copy of the manifest reaches the authorities after receiving the hazardous waste from the occupier/generator. The owner/operator should indicate the proposed treatment and disposal scheme to be followed for the hazardous waste. The copy of the manifest should be linked with the copy of the manifest sent by the occupier/generator.

Noise Pollution Norms

Noise is defined as unwanted sound. Sound which pleases the listeners is music and that which causes pain and annoyance is noise. At times what is music for some can be noise for others.
Most of the machines that have been developed for industrial purposes, for high speed transportation, or to make life more enjoyable, by furnishing additional comfort, reducing the drudgery of everyday living, and speeding up our daily routines to provide additional leisure hours, are accompanied by noise. Noise prevention and control is important as noise affects us in hearing, ability to communicate and behaviour. Undoubtedly, lesser noise can make the environment more friendly and life becomes pleasant.

Sources of Noise

Various sources of noise are : industry, road traffic, rail traffic, air traffic, construction and public works, indoor sources(air conditioners, air coolers, radio, television and other home appliances) etc. In Indian conditions, indiscriminate use of public address system and DG sets, has given a new dimension to the noise pollution problem.

Standards and Guidelines

- The Central Pollution Control Board constituted a Committee on Noise Pollution Control. The Committee recommended noise standards for ambient air and for automobiles, domestic appliances and construction equipments, which were later notified in Environment (Protection) Rules,1986 as given below:

Area Code	Category of Area	Limits in dB (A), Leq Day time	Night time
A	Industrial area	75	70
B	Commercial area	65	55
C	Residential area	55	45
D	Silence Zone	50	40

Notes:

1. Day time is reckoned in between 6 a.m. and 9 p.m.
2. Night time is reckoned in between 9 p.m. and 6 a.m.
3 .Silence zone is referred as areas upto 100 meters around such premises as hospitals, educational institutions and courts. The Silence zones are to be declared by the Competent Authority.

Use of vehicular horns, loudspeakers and bursting of crackers shall be banned in these zones.

4. Mixed categories of areas should be declared as one of the four above mentioned categories by the Competent Authority and the corresponding standards shall apply.

- Noise standards for automobiles, domestic appliances and construction equipments have been notified in Part 'E', Schedule-VI of Environment (Protection) Rules, 1986, as amended on 19th May, 1993, as given in the tables below.

Category of Vehicle	Noise limit in db(A)
(a) Motorcycle, scooters and three Wheelers.	80
(b) Passenger Cars	82
(c) Passenger or commercial vehicles up to 4 MT	85
(d) Passenger or commercial vehicles above 4 MT and upto 12 MT	89
(e) Passenger or commercial vehicles exceeding 12 MT	91

Category of Domestic Appliances/ Construction Equipments	Noise limits in dB(A)
(a) Window air conditioners of 1 tone to 1.5 tone	68
(b) Air Coolers	60
(c) Refrigerators	46
(d) Diesel Generator for domestic purposes	85-90
(e) Compactors (rollers), Front loaders, Concrete mixers, Cranes (movable), Vibrators and Saws	75

The Noise Pollution Control Committee also prescribed code of practice for controlling noise from sources other than industries and automobiles, as given below:

Code of practice for Controlling Noise from Sources other than Industries and Automobiles

Public Address System

- License must be obtained by all parties intending to use loudspeakers or public address system for any occasion.
- Public address system and loudspeakers should not be used at night between 9 p.m. to 6 a.m. except in closed premises.
- Loudspeakers should be directed at the audiences and not away from audience (i.e. not towards the neighbourhoods).
- Loudspeakers should not be allowed for advertisement and commercial activities.
- The permitted strength of power amplifier should be just adequate to cover the audience, and noise level beyond the boundary limit of the noise source premises should not be increased by more than 5 dB(A) above the ambient noise level.

Aircraft Operations

- Aerodrome should be located away from the city and growth of the city should not be allowed to extend upto the Aerodrome.
- Aeroplanes should take off in direction radially away from the city.

- During boarding and unboarding operations the plane should be sufficiently away from the airport buildings.
- Night-time operations should be minimised.
- During maintenance and repairs of the aeroplane, workers should use ear muffs.
- Portable silencers should be used in the plane intake as well as exhaust during idling period at the airport.

Railway Operations

- Erection of acoustic barrier, reducing speed and avoiding whistling within and along the municipal limits and habitation zones are recommended for adoption to the extent possible.

Construction Activities

- Acoustic barriers should be placed near construction sites.
- The maximum noise levels near the construction site should be limited to 75 dB (A) Leq (5 min.) in industrial areas and to 65 dB(A) Leq (5 min.) in other areas.
- There should be fencing around the construction site to prevent people coming near the site.
- Materials need not be stockpiled and unused equipment to be placed between noisy operating equipments and other areas.
- Constructing temporary earth bund around the site using soil etc. which normally is hauled away from the construction site.

Burning of Crackers

- Manufacture and sale of crackers having an impulsive noise having an impulsive noise of more than 90 dB at 5 meters distance from the site of bursting should be banned.
- Manufacture and bursting of joined crackers should be banned.
- Bursting of crackers during night between 9 p.m. and 6 a.m. should be banned.
- Bursting of crackers may be permitted only during public festivals.

The permissible levels for noise exposure for work zone area have been prescribed under the Model Rules of the Factories Act, 1948, as given in the Tables below.

Peak sound pressure level in dB	Permitted number of impulses or impact/day
140	100
135	315
130	1,000
125	3,160
120	10,000

Notes:

1. No exposure in excess of 140 dB peak sound pressure level is permitted.

2. For any peak sound pressure level falling in between any figure and the next higher or lower figure as indicated in column 1, the permitted number of impulses or impacts per day is to be determined by extrapolation on a proportionate basis.

Total time of exposure (continuous or a number of short term exposures) per day, in hr	Sound pressure level in dB(A)
8	90
6	92
4	95
3	97
2	100
1-1/2	102
1	105
1/2	107
1/4	110
1/8	115

Notes:

1. No exposure in excess of 115 dB(A) is to be permitted.

2. For any period of exposure falling in between any figure and the next higher or lower figure as indicated in column 1, the permissible sound pressure level is to be determined by extrapolation on a proportionate basis.

Guidelines for Adoption of Clean Technology

Economic development of any nation depends upon several factors such as energy production and conservation: raw materials like water, minerals, forest produce and capability and skill to manage the resources optimally. Adoption of cleaner modes of production helps in resource conservation and elimination of gaseous, liquid or solid wastes.

Clean technology therefore entails:

- waste prevention and reduction by reduced consumption of raw materials,
- modification and up gradation of the technological processes so that optimal utilization of natural resources is made possible,
- adoption of preventive rather than corrective approaches to pollution control

To encourage identification, acquisition, development and promotion of cleaner technologies at all levels, a network of clean technology centres need to be set up, with a National Centre coordinating their activities. A centre for clean technology should be able to carry out the following:

- identify the areas where introduction of clean technologies is possible;
- identify the source(s) from where clean technology and data/details thereof can be obtained;
- assess the technology available indigenously as well as those to be imported;
- modify the technology, if necessary and demonstrate it to the satisfaction of the users so that it can be replicated;
- undertake Research and Development to develop technologies for cleaner production;
- collect, collate and disseminate information on clean technology; and
- maintain interaction with the industry, financial institutions and Research and Development Laboratories for adoption of clean technologies.

Discussion with the concerned Central Government departments, industry associations, research organisations and financial institutions have recommended the setting up of a sectoral clean Technology Centre dealing with coal mining, beneficiation, transportation, utilisation and waste disposal at the earliest.

In the pulp and paper manufacturing sector, several clean technologies such as anaerobic treatment, lignin recovery etc. can be adopted for pulp and paper production as the success of these efforts has been established with pilot plant tests. Other examples of clean technologies relate to:

- use of lignin to develop value added products.
- use of flyash generated during burning of lignin for brick-making.
- reduction in raw material consumption.

Plans are under preparation to initiate "Demonstration Projects" for promotion of cleaner modes of production in selected areas, as a large number of industrial units in our country are 35 - 40 years old and are ready to be discarded or upgraded and may therefore persuaded to switch over to clean technologies.

Environmental Impact Assessment (EIA)

1. The purpose of Environmental Impact Assessment (EIA) is to identify and evaluate the potential impacts (beneficial and adverse) of development and projects on the environmental system. It is an useful aid for decision making based on understanding of the environment implications including social, cultural and aesthetic concerns which could be integrated with the analysis of the project costs and benefits. This exercise should be undertaken early enough in the planning stage of projects for selection of environmentally compatible sites, process technologies and such other environmental safeguards.
2. While all industrial projects may have some environmental impacts all of them may not be significant enough to warrant elaborate assessment procedures. The need for such exercises

will have to be decided after initial evaluation of the possible implications of a particular project and its location. The projects which could be the candidates for detailed Environment Impact Assessment include the following:

- Those which can significantly alter the landscape, land use pattern and lead to concentration of working and service population;
- Those which need upstream development activity like assured mineral and forest products supply or downstream industrial process development;
- Those involving manufacture, handling and use of hazardous materials;
- Those which are sited near ecologically sensitive areas, urban centres, hill resorts, places of scientific and religious importance.
- Industrial Estates with constituent units of various types which could cumulatively cause significant environmental damage.

3. The Environmental Impact Assessment (EIA) should be prepared on the basis of the existing background pollution levels vis-à-vis contributions of pollutants from the proposed plant. The EIA should address some of the basic factors listed below:

- Meteorology and air quality

Ambient levels of pollutants such as Sulphur Dioxide, oxides of nitrogen, carbon monoxide, suspended particulate matters, should be determined at the centre and at 3 other locations on a radius of 10 km with 120 degrees angle between stations. Additional contribution of pollutants at the locations are required to be predicted after taking into account the emission rates of the pollutants from the stacks of the proposed plant, under different meteorological conditions prevailing in the area.

- Hydrology and water quality
- Site and its surroundings
- Occupational safety and health

- Details of the treatment and disposal of effluents(liquid, air and solid) and the methods of alternative uses
- Transportation of raw material and details of material handling
- Control equipment and measures proposed to be adopted

4. Preparation of Environmental Management Plan is required for formulation, implementation and monitoring of environmental protection measures during and after commissioning of projects.

Environmental Guidelines for Industries

In order to help the concerned authorities and the entrepreneurs, it is necessary to frame certain broad guidelines for sitting an industry. It is also necessary to identify the parameters that should be taken into account while setting up an industry. With this in view, the following environmental guidelines are recommended for sitting of Industries to ensure optimum use of natural and man-made resources in sustainable manner with minimal depletion, degradation and/or destruction of environment. Those are in addition to those directives that are already in existence under the Industries (Development and Regulation) Act.

Areas to be Avoided

In sitting industries, care should be taken to minimise the adverse impact of the industries on the immediate neighbourhood as well as distant places. Some of the natural life sustaining systems and some specific land uses are sensitive to industrial impacts because of the nature and extent of fragility. With a view to protecting such an industrial sites shall maintain the following distances from the areas listed:

- Ecologically and/or otherwise sensitive areas: at least 25 km; depending on the geo-climatic conditions the requisite distance hall have to be increased by the appropriate agency.
- Coastal areas: at least 1/2 km from High Tide Line.

- Flood Plain of the Riverine Systems: at least 1/2 km from flood plain or modified flood plain affected by dam in the upstream or by flood control systems.
- Transport/Communication System: at least 1/2 km from highway and railway.
- Major settlements (3, 00,000 population): distance from settlements is difficult to maintain because of urban sprawl. At the time of sitting of the industry if any major settlement's notified limit is within 50 km, the spatial direction of growth of the settlement for at least a decade must be assessed and the industry shall be sited at least 25 km from the projected growth boundary of the settlement.

Pre-requisite: State and Central Governments are required to identify such areas on a priority basis.

Note: Ecological and/or otherwise sensitive areas include

- Religious and Historic Places;
- Archaeological Monuments (e.g. identified zone around Taj Mahal);
- Scenic Areas;
- Hill Resorts;
- Beach Resorts;
- Health Resorts;
- Coastal Areas rich in Coral, Mangroves, Breeding Grounds of Specific Species;
- Estuaries rich in Mangroves, Breeding Ground of Specific Species;
- Gulf Areas;
- Biosphere Reserves;
- National Parks and Sanctuaries;
- Natural Lakes, Swamps;
- Seismic Zones;
- Tribal Settlements;
- Areas of Scientific and Geological interest;
- Defence Installations, specially those of security importance and sensitive to pollution;

- Border Areas (International) and
- Airports.

Sitting Criteria

Economic and social factors are recognized and assessed while sitting an industry. Environmental factors must be taken into consideration in industrial sitting. Proximity of water sources, highway, major settlements, markets for products and raw material resources is desired for economy of production, but all the above listed systems must be away for environmental protection. Industries are, therefore, required to be sited, striking a balance between economic and environmental considerations. In such a selected site, the following factors must be recognized.

- No forest land shall be converted into non-forest activity for the sustenance of the industry (Ref: Forest Conservation Act, 1980).
- No prime agricultural land shall be converted into industrial site.
- Within the acquired site the industry must locate itself at the lowest location to remain obscured from general sight.
- Land acquired shall be sufficiently large to provide space for appropriate treatment of waste water still left for treatment after maximum possible reuse and recycle. Reclaimed (treated) wastewater shall be used to raise green belt and to create water body for aesthetics, recreation and if possible, for aquaculture. The green belt shall be 1/2 km wide around the battery limit of the industry. For industry having odour problem it shall be a kilometer wide.
- The green belt between two adjoining large scale industries shall be one kilometer.
- Enough space should be provided for storage of solid wastes so that these could be available for possible reuse.
- Lay out and form of the industry that may come up in the area must conform to the landscape of the area without affecting the scenic features of that place.

- Associated township of the industry must be created at a space having physiographic barrier between the industry and the township.
- Each industry is required to maintain three ambient air quality measuring stations within 120 degree angle between stations.

Sitting Guidelines for Industries

- Industrial development significantly contributes towards economic growth. However, industrial progress brings along with it a host of environmental problems. Many of these problems could be avoided if industries are located on the basis of environmental considerations, injudicious sitting of industry can seriously affect the environmental features such as air, water, land, flora, fauna, human settlements and health of people. The entrepreneur should be fully aware of these implications and he should take necessary steps while setting up the industry so as to minimise the possible adverse effects on the environmental resources and quality of life. Often, an entrepreneur finds it very costly to install pollution control equipment and other mitigative measures after the industry is already set up. As such, preventive steps are needed at the time of sitting rather than going in for curative measures at a later stage.
- The Industrial Policy Statement of July 1980, recognised the need for preserving ecological balance and improving living conditions in the urban centres of the country. On the basis of this Policy, indiscriminate expansion of the existing industries and setting up of new industrial undertakings within the limits of metropolitan cities and the larger towns should not be permitted. However, the Policy has not touched upon the implications of setting up an industry in sensitive areas, both ecological and otherwise, which would have an affection the overall development process.
- At present, industries are being located on the basis of raw material availability, access to the market, transport facilities and such other techno-economic considerations without

adequate attention to environmental considerations are recognised as an important criterion for setting of industry.

- To prevent, air, water and soil pollution arising out of industrial projects, the industrial Licensing procedure requires that the entrepreneurs before setting up the industry obtain clearance from Central/State Air and Water Pollution Control Boards. The Central State Pollution Control Boards stipulate that air (gases) and water (effluents) emanating from the industry should adhere to certain quality standards. However, these stipulations do not prevent the industry from effecting the total environment by wrong sitting. Also, the cumulative effect of a number of industries at a particular place is not being studied upon, with the result that an industry or an industrial area over a period of time could cause significant damage to the surrounding environment and ecological features.
- In respect of certain industrial development projects it is not only necessary to install suitable pollution control equipment but also to identify appropriate sites for their location. To give a concrete shape to this requirement, a select group of 20 industries has been notified by the Department of Industrial Development. A formalised procedure has been stipulated for site selection from environment angle with regard to these projects.
- According to this procedure for the select group of industries, the letters of intent should be converted to industrial licences only after the following conditions have been fulfilled:

➢ The State Director of Industries confirms that the site of the project has been approved from environmental angle by the competent State Authority.

➢ The entrepreneur commits both to the State Government and Central Government that he will install the appropriate equipment and implement the prescribed measures for the prevention and control of pollution.

➢ The concerned State Pollution Control Board has certified that the proposal meets with the environmental requirements and that the equipment installed or proposed to be installed are adequate and appropriate to the requirement.

- The State Department of Environment will be the competent authority for approval of project sites from environmental angle. In those States where such Departments have not yet been set up, approval should be obtained from the nodal agency designated for looking after environmental matters. With regard to projects where support from the Central Government/International Agencies is envisaged and which come under the purview of Industrial Licensing, approval of the project site from environmental angle should be obtained from the Ministry of Environment and Forests, Government of India. The entrepreneur should provide the details of proposed project site, pollution abatement measures and such other relevant information as required for review from environmental angle.
- The entrepreneur wills bee required to submit half-yearly progress report on installation of pollution control devices to the respective State Pollution Control Boards.
- Depending on the nature and location of the project, the entrepreneur will be required to submit comprehensive Report, and Environment Management Plans.

Bibliography

Select Bibliography

Reports/Government Documents

Basant, Sunila–Confidential Report No – 1247 sent to the Commissioner and Secretary, Home Department, Old Secretariat, June 5, Patna, 1982. This report was filed in the Supreme Court of India in connection with writ petition Nos 371-75 of 1983.

Centre for Science and Environment (CSE)–The First Citizen's Report, New Delhi, 1982.

Centre for Science and Environment (CSE)–The State of India's Environment: The Second Citizen's Report, New Delhi, 1985.

Government of Bihar–Suberna Rekha Multipurpose Project, Irrigation Department, Patna.

World Commission on Environment and Development, Our Common Future, Oxford University Press, New Delhi, 1987.

Books

Abraham, M. Francis (ed.)–Studies in Third World Development, Deep and Deep, New Delhi, 1992.

Agarwal, Anil, Darryl D'Monte and Ujwala Samarth–The fight for Survival: People's Action for Environment, Centre for Science and Environment, New Delhi, 1987.

Agarwal, Anil and Sunita Narain–Towards a Green World: Should Global Environmental Management be Built on Legal Conventions or Human Rights?, Centre for Science and Environment, New Delhi, 1992.

Amin, Shahid–Event, Metaphor, Memory: Chauri Chaura 1922-1992, Oxford University Press, Delhi – 1996.

Anna da Soledade vierra–Environmental Information in Developing Nations, Greenwood Press, London, 1985.

Arvill–Man and Environment, Penguin Press, London, 1977.

Arvind Anjum–Subernarekha Ka Aahvan, Visthapith Mukti Vahini, Singhbhum.

Asthana, Vandana–The Politics of Environment: A profile, Ashish Publishing House, Delhi, 1992.

Bahuguna, Sunderlal, Vandana Shiva and M. N. Buch–Environment crisis and Sustainable Development, Natraj Publishers, Dehra Dun, 1992.

Baviskar, Amita–In the Belly of the River, Oxford University Press, New Delhi, 1995.

Centre for Science and Environment (CSE)–Proceedings of the Seminar on Traditional Water Harvesting System in India, October 9-11, New Delhi, 1990.

Daniel M. Dworkin–Environmental Sciences in Developing Countries, USA, 1974.

__ Environment and Development, USA, 1974.

Desai, Bharat–Water Pollution in India: Law and Enforcement, Lancers, New Delhi, 1990.

Dickson, D.–Alternative Technology, Fontana, London, 1977.

D'Monte, Darryl–Temples or Tombs, Centre for Science and Environment, New Delhi, 1985.

Fedorov, E., Man and Nature, Progress, Moscow, 1980.

Gadgil, Madhav and Ramchandra Guha–This Fissured Land: An Ecological History of India, Oxford University Press, New Delhi, 1992.

Gandhi, Mahatma–Hind Swaraj, Navjivan, Ahmedabad, 1962.

Guha, Ramchandra, The Unquiet Woods: Ecological Change and Peasant Resistance in the Himalayas, Oxford University Press, New Delhi, 1989.

Hemant and Ranjeev–Jab Nadi Bandi, Jay Prabha Aadhyayan Avam Anusandhan Kendra, Madhupur, 1991.

Hirsch, Philip–'Dammed or Damned? Hydropower versus People's power', Bulletin of Concerned Asian Scholars, vol. XX, No-1, 1988.

Kneese, A.V.–Economics and the Environment, Penguin, Harmondsworth, 1977.

Kohli, Atul–The State and Poverty in India : The Politics Of Reform, Cambridge University Press, Cambridge, 1987.

Kothari, Rajni–Rethinking Development, In Search Of Humane Alternatives, Ajanta Publications, 1988.

—- State against Democracy, Ajanta, New Delhi, 1988.

—- Politics and the People (2 vols.), Ajanta, New Delhi, 1989.

Mc Cormick, John–The Global Environmental Movement, Belhaven Press, London, 1989.

Mohan, I. (ed.)–The Fragile Environment, Ashish Publishing House, New Delhi, 1997.

Prem Prabhakar–Hum Sari Duniya Badlenge, Jay Prabha Aadyayan Avam Anusandhan Kendra, Madhupur.

Redclift, Michael–Sustainable Development: Exploring the Contradictions, Methuen, London,1987.

—Development and the Environmental Crisis: Red or Green Alternatives?, Methuen, London, 1984.

Revelle Penelope and Revelle Charles–The Environment Issues and Choices for Society, D. Van Nostrand Company, New York, 1981.

Sapru, R.K. (ed)–Environmental Management in India, Ashish Publishing House, New Delhi, 1987.

Sapru, R.K. and Shyama Bhardwaj (ed.)–The New Environmental Age, Ashish Publishing House, New Delhi, 1990.

Sax, J.L.–Defending the Environment: A handbook for Citizen Action, Vintage Books, New York, 1970.

Schumacher, E.F.–Small is Beautiful: A Study of Economics As If People Mattered, Blond and Briggs, London, 1973.

Sengupta, Nirmal–Managing Common Property: Irrigation in India and the Philippines, Sage, New Delhi, 1991.

Singh, Ram Bali (ed.)–Study in Environment and Development, Commonwealth Publications, New Delhi, 1988.

Vakil, Arun C.–Environmental Issues in India, Commerce Publications Division, Bombay, 1979.

Von oppen, M; etal–Alternative for Improving Small Scale Irrigation Systems in Alfisols watersheds in India, Water Management and Policy Work, Khon Kaen, Thailand, September, 1983.

Watt, K.E.F.–Understanding the Environment, USA, 1982.

Yogendra and Safdar Imam Kadari–Ganga Ko Abiral Bahane Do, Ganga Mukti Andolan Publication, Bhagalpur, 1990.

Articles

Aloysius, Raj–'Kharkai Bandh Ban Jane Se Kolhan Ka Astitva Hi Mit Jayega', Singhbhum Ekta, Vol. VIII, No-10, December 21, 1985.

Areeparampil, Mathew–'The Impact of Subernarekha Multipurpose Project On the Indigenous People of Singhbhum' People and Dams, Society for Participatory Research in Asia, New Delhi.

Chandra, Sudhir–To my successor, in The Times of India: Sunday Review, November 8, 1987.

Chandresh–Nadi Per Zamindari: Jal Mein Machali Ke Bajaye Machuare, Dinman, July 3-9, 1983.

Dasgupta, Saibal–'Pollution Persists in the Ganga near Varanasi', The Times of India, September 19, 1992.

Dandekar, V. M. and N. Rath–Poverty in India, Economic and Political Weekly, January 1971.

Dasgupta, Biplab–The Environment Debate: Some Issues and Trends, Economic and Political Weekly, Annual 1978.

Dhanagare, D. and J. John–Cyclical Movement Towards the Eternal: Nine Theses of Social Movements: A Critique, Economic and Political Weekly, May 21, 1988.

D'Monte, Darryl–Ecology vs. the Economy in India, New Leader, May 1982.

Dogra, Bharat–Environment Protection: Myths and Reality, The Financial Express, New Delhi, July 27, 1991.

Fernandes, Paul–'Subernarekha Multipurpose Project: Towards Evolving a Strategy for the Management of Displaced Families, XLRI, Jamshedpur, 1985.

Frank, Andre Gunder and Marta Fuentes–'Nine Theses on Social Movements, Economic and Political Weekly, August 29, 1987

Guha, Ramchandra, 'Ideological Trends in Indian Environmentalism', Economic and Political Weekly, vol.23, no.49, December 3, 1988.

— 'The Problem', Seminar, Special Issue on New Social Movements, no.355, 1989.

—'Prehistory of Indian Environmentalism–Intellectual Traditions', Economic and Political Weekly, January 4-11, 1992.

— 'Social-Ecological Research in India–A status Report', Economic and Political Weekly, February 15, 1997.

Huq, Masoodul–'How the Police Killed a War Hero', Sunday, vol. IX, No-49, May 23-29, 1982.

Jha, I.M.–'Subernarekha Project to have Two Barrages', The Indian Nation, Patna, September 4, 1981.

Khoshoo, T. N.–Ecology Must Blend with Economy, The Times of India, New Delhi, January 4, 1992.

Kothari, Rajni 'The Non-Party Political Process', Economic and Political Weekly, February 4, 1984.

Kothari, Smitu–Ecology vs Development: The Struggle for Survival, Social Action, October-December, 1985.

Omvedt, Gail–'Ecology and Social Movements', Economic and Political Weekly, November 3, 1984.

Patankar, Bharat–'Monochromatic Green Gathering', Race and Class, vol.31, No.2, 1989.

Rai, Usha–Saving The Environment, The Indian Express, New Delhi, March 30, 1992.

Sengupta, Nirmal, 'The Indigenous Irrigation Organization in South Bihar', The Indian Economic and Social History Review, vol.XVII, No.2, 1982.

Seth, D.L.–'Movements', Seminar, October, No.278, 1982.

— 'Grass-roots Initiatives in India', Economic and Political Weekly, February 11, 1982.

Sethi, Harsh–'Groups in a New Politics of Transformation', Economic and Political Weekly, February 18, 1984.

Sharma, Kalpana–Who is to Pay for the Clean Up? The Hindu, New Delhi, April 10, 1992.

Sharma, Aneeta–' Ganga fish a health hazard', The Times of India, March 12, 2001.

Sharma, Mukul–A struggle for fishing rights', Frontline, July 16, 1999.

Singh, Shekhar–'Some Aspects of the Ecological Crisis in India, Social Scientist, 1985.

Swain, Ashok–'Democratic Consolidation? Environmental Movements in India, Asian Survey, September 1997.

Index

Index